A SHORT DICTIONARY OF ANGLO-SAXON POETRY

A SHORT
DICTIONARY
OF
ANGLO-SAXON
POETRY

*In a Normalized
Early West-Saxon Orthography*

J. B. BESSINGER

*University College
University of Toronto*

UNIVERSITY OF TORONTO PRESS

Preface

THIS DICTIONARY is based primarily on the text of *The Anglo-Saxon Poetic Records* (edd. George P. Krapp and Elliott V. K. Dobbie, New York, 1931–1953), with additional references adjusted to other modern editions of individual poems. It is a gloss to the crucial 40 per cent of the poetic vocabulary—some 3000 parent words, mostly simplex forms, that are the basic units of a markedly synthetic diction. The remainder, largely unglossed in this dictionary, is built according to transparent principles upon the compounding of parent words, and the resulting compounds are with some exceptions self-explanatory. The exceptional compounds of special meaning are glossed in this book along with parent words. Cross-references are given to the forms of verbs, adjectives, and adverbs which are most commonly troublesome to the student. In all, the dictionary contains about 5000 entries, many of which include additional compounded forms. Excluded from it are most unassimilated Hebrew, Greek, and Latin words, most proper names, and inflected forms of the definite article and the pronouns, except when these form homographs with other glossed words.

The first aim of the dictionary is to be useful to those reading the poetry in the normalized texts edited by Francis P. Magoun, Jr.: *Anglo-Saxon Poems* (Department of English, Harvard University, 1956, 1960), *Béowulf and Judith* (1959), *The Vercelli Book Poems* (1960). I have tried, however, to bring together a basic normalized vocabulary of the complete poetic corpus (not merely that of the normalized poems in print at this date) and to make the list as broadly useful as was feasible within modest limits. Included with each head-word is such brief grammatical information as will most likely seem helpful to the student. The spelling and diacritical markings adopted here, as in the Magoun editions, should also encourage the student to read the poetry aloud with some confidence—with too much, perhaps, if he imagines that any Anglo-Saxon ever wrote or pronounced a "pure" dialect. But this poetry, of formative oral tradition and lasting oral effectiveness, must above all be sounded; the pleasure it gives as poetry may then lead to more various and less confident grammatical, dialectal, or paleographical studies.

The normalized Early West-Saxon orthography here used follows, with a few theoretical and typographical modifications, Ferdinand Holthausen's *Altenglisches etymologisches Wörterbuch* (Heidelberg, 1934), and can be used as a guide from un-normalized texts and lexicons to the historical and comparative information in that work via the normalized texts translated in this medium.

Each head-word is cross-referenced to *A Grouped Frequency Word-List of Anglo-Saxon Poetry*, by John F. Madden, C.S.B. and Francis P. Magoun, Jr. (Department of English, Harvard University, 1957, 1960). The user of the dictionary can therefore refer quickly to the *Word-List* for systematic study and memorizing of words and word-clusters; or, without reference to the *Word-List*, recognize the words of high frequency relationships (the range is from unique occurrences to 15974) which must be learned early.[1]

The brevity of the present dictionary is made possible by the assumption of the reader's knowledge of compounding principles, an outline of which is given below; if he has also mastered the word-groups of highest frequency, he will be spared the tedium of searching out two or more head-words for each untranslated compound, and can still preserve his duty and right to translate each compound afresh upon recognizing its elements. Needless to say, the entries here do not offer the advanced student the subtle and richly annotated definitions available to him in glossed texts and larger dictionaries. I hope the book will be permanently useful to him, however, as a normalized key to the basic vocabulary. Since the reconstruction of compounds is left so largely to the reader's adventurous intuition, the distinction between (unglossed) transparent and (glossed) opaque compounds is critical, and has some-times been hard to make. I have followed an inclination to be puzzled easily and included some compounds that will seem transparent to others. These will hardly be in the way, and may be treated merely as examples of compounding patterns, unless they are also to be challenged for their definitions; a likely enough event, in view of what Dr. Kenneth Sisam calls "the characteristic imprecision of the language of Old English verse, where general terms are preferred, roughly synonymous ex-pressions are accumulated, and compounds of vague meaning are freely used."[2]

I owe to Professor Magoun the reminder that the alphabetical arrangements of Old English dictionaries and glossaries are perhaps needlessly (and comparatively) inconvenient, as a result of attempts to weave into the Latin alphabet the special additional characters used by the scribes. In this book I have gratefully followed his suggestion and the example of the Scandinavian dictionaries and removed [þ], [æ], and [œ] to the end of the ordinary alphabet; the crossed *d* or "eth" character, never initial in the present orthography, follows the ordinary *d*. This arrangement should recommend itself for its consistency and for the secondary convenience of aligning Old English with Old Norse and Modern Icelandic dictionaries.

The debt of this book to the work of others is very great, first to the editors and authors of the poetic texts, lexicons, grammars, and special studies on which it depends, and next most especially to my friends Father Madden and Professor Magoun, of whose *Word-List* the present dictionary began as a revised alphabetiza-

---

[1]Members of the first 1000 word-groups, printed in the *Word-List* within 35 pages of large type, comprise 90 per cent of the words used in the poetry. It should perhaps be stressed that grouped frequency numbers do not always indicate high frequency in a given word, but rather in that word together with its relatives, if any: Anglo-Saxon "and" meaning *and* has an absolute frequency of 5001; "mennisc" *human* is rare in the poetry, but owes its high frequency number (1030) to its membership in a group with "mann" *human being*. For a discussion of frequency principles and of the normalized orthography here used, see the *Word-List*, "Foreword," pp. iii-xi, where there is also a useful set of normalized grammatical paradigms for the beginner. Historical and pragmatic discussions of normal-ization are to be found in Charles L. Wrenn, " 'Standard' Old English," *Transactions of the Philo-logical Society* (1933), 65–88, and Francis P. Magoun, Jr., "A Brief Plea for a Normalization of Old-English Poetical Texts," *Les Langues Modernes*, XLV (1951), 63–69. The frequency data quoted above are taken from the *Word-List* and from John F. Madden, "A Frequency Word-Count of Anglo-Saxon Poetry," *Mediaeval Studies*, XV (1953), 221–225.

[2]*The Review of English Studies*, IX (1958), 132. Cp. Charles L. Wrenn, ed., *Beowulf* (London, 1953, 1958), p. 82: "The only rule one can propose is that the student should always satisfy his conscience before translating the compound that he knows clearly the literal meaning of each element."

tion. They not only allowed this use of their work but gave generous counsel in the planning of the dictionary. Father Madden, with Professor Donald F. Chapin, also helped me through many months of the first stages of compilation and checking, and Professor Magoun, finally, has read proofs. I owe them all warm thanks, and the same go to the Director, Editor, and staff of the University of Toronto Press for their patient encouragement and skill in planning and production.

J.B.B.

University College, Toronto

On Compounding and Modification

THE LISTING of compounds or secondary formations in the dictionary is minimal, although a number of compounds are listed which seem important enough to be considered virtually as parent or primary words: Anglo-Saxon "módiʒ", meaning *bold*, wís-dóm *wisdom*, etc. But in general transparent compounds are excluded, for their possible permutations are many and their meanings obvious as the sum of their parts: módiʒ-líće *boldly*, dóm-dæʒ *judgment day*, etc. Compounds whose meanings for various reasons do not appear to equal the sum of their parts will most often be found in the dictionary: gár-secg *stormy* (?) *ocean*, mearg-cofa *marrow-chamber*, i.e. *bone*, etc.

The student will, to be sure, notice peculiarities of meaning and structure that lead him beyond the basic compounding principles outlined below, into linguistic decisions on one hand and poetic criticism on the other. He will meet words with differing though related meanings: dóm *judgment*; *power*; *glory*; weorc *work, action*; *hardship, grief*; etc. Some words of general meaning may of course have a limited meaning in a given context: stígan *go, move*; á-stígan *ascend* or *descend* as the context requires. In all such cases the poetic context is the best guide, but sample entries in the dictionary will be found helpful. The same is true of homographs in composition: ǽ *law*, ǽ- *privative prefix*, "*without*"; ǽ-lǽrend *doctor of the law*, ǽ-menn *uninhabited*. Less demanding of the reader, since the resulting compound is always recognizable, is the irregular appearance of a final vowel (i.e. loss of final *-a, -e, -u,* or addition of a final *-e*) in the first element of a compound: æðele *noble*, æðel-cund *of noble origin*; ćearu *care*, ćear-wielm *surge of grief*; hell *hell*, hell-cræft *diabolical art*, helle-fýr *hell-fire*; scucca *demon*, scucc-ʒield *idol*; etc.

The structure of compounds, however, is on the whole very regular; only their poetic complexity is variable and therefore challenging. Some compounds are tautological: bed-ræst *bed*; dǽd-weorc *deed, work, action*; gum-mann *man*; mód-sefa *mind*; sǽ-holm *sea*. Conversely, some go so far as to intensify the separate elements by rime: borg-sorg *the sorrow that comes from borrowing*: héah-fréa *supreme lord*; héah-þréa *extreme terror*; nearu-searu *secret cunning*; sand-land *sandy shore*; waroþ-faroþ *shore-wave, surf*; word-hord *word-hoard*. Compounds may be literal in meaning: drinc-fæt *drinking vessel*; fisc-nett *fish-net*; heofon-hróf *roof of heaven*; múþ-bana *one who kills with his mouth*; sǽ-cyning *sea-king*. Or they may be figurative, often elaborately so: gréot-hord *dust-hoard*, i.e. *treasure to be kept (in the grave) by the earth*, i.e. *body*; hord-fæt *treasure-vessel*, i.e. *Mary's womb*; mere-hræʒl *sea-garment*, i.e. *sail*; weorold-candel *world-candle*, i.e. *sun*. A good many are ambiguously literal or figurative: bán-fæt *bone-vessel*, i.e. *body*, whether intended as a metaphor or as a quasi-realistic description; déaþ-bedd *death-bed*, but in its unique occurrence meaning only *place of death*; heall-þeʒn *hall-retainer*, used literally and also ironically to mean *(wrongful) occupant of the hall*; gold-ʒiefa *gold-giver*, i.e. *lord*, perhaps best translated

viii

generous lord; gold-hord *precious treasure*, used literally and also to mean *Christ* and *the Cross*; gold-wine *gold-friend*, i.e. (*generous*) *lord*; sǽ-láf *what is left by the sea*, i.e. in its unique occurrence (*booty*) *left by the sea* or *survivor of the sea*; ýþ-láf *what is left by waves, sand*, i.e. *shore*.

In the examples given it will be seen that the first element of the compound modifies the second. This is also true of other than nominal compounds; verbs, for example, are frequently modified by prefixes: bindan *bind*, on-bindan *unbind*; winnan *struggle*, ȝe-winnan *win*.

Equally common is the formation of new words by means of suffixes: blód *blood*, blódiȝ *bloody*; gód *good*, gód-ness *goodness*.

A selective outline of compounding principles now follows.

A. Nominal and Adjectival Compounding

The compounding and modification of a parent word: mód *mind, heart, soul; courage, pride, greatness* (grouped poetic frequency 840)

1 (*a*) Noun + noun = noun: mód-cræft *skill*, mód-ȝe-þanc *thought*, mód-hete *hate*, mód-hord (*mind's treasury of*) *thought*, mód-lufu *love*, mód-sorg *sorrow*.

   (*b*) Noun or adjective + noun = adjective: gúþ-mód *warlike, fierce in spirit*,[1] ierre-mód *angry*, léoht-mód *cheerful*, rúm-mód *gracious, liberal*, wráþ-mód *wrathful*.

2. Adjective or adverb + adjective = adjective: éaþ-mœ́de *mild*, fela-módiȝ *very brave*, ofer-módiȝ *proud*, til-módiȝ *noble-minded, virtuous*, wiðer-mœ́de *antagonistic*.

3. Noun + adjective = adjective: mód-blind *unperceiving*, mód-blissiende *joyful*, mód-ćeariȝ *anxious*, mód-full *arrogant*, mód-gléaw *wise*, mód-glæd *happy*, mód-hwæt *bold*,[2] mód-léof *beloved*, mód-séoc *distressed*, mód-swíþ *resolute*.

4 (*a*) Adjective + noun = noun: [No clear examples occur with this parent word, but the formation is common: gód-dǽd *benefit*, héah-cyning *great king*, láþ-spell *grievous news*, sóþ-cwide *true saying*.]

   (*b*) Adjective + noun = adjective: déor-mód *brave*, forht-mód *frightened*, gléaw-mód *wise*, glæd-mód *happy*, héah-mód *exultant*, héan-mód *dejected*, hwæt-mód *bold*, miċel-mód *magnanimous*, swíþ-mód *stout-hearted, magnanimous, haughty, violent*,[3] torht-mód *illustrious*, wœ́riȝ-mód *despondent*.

5 (*a*) Adverb + noun = noun: éaþ-mœ́du *humility*, ofer-mód *overconfidence*, ofer-mœ́de *pride*.

[1] The modifying element (gúþ-) is possibly an example of the "horrific intensive": this element, representing ideas of hostility, terror, death, and the like, modifies the second element with these connotations. Similar are: beadu- *war*, heaðu- *battle*, heoru- *sword*, inwit- *malice*, wæl- *slaughter*, wíȝ- *war*. See Ernst A. Kock, "Old West Germanic and Old Norse," *Studies in English Philology: A Miscellany in Honor of Frederick Klaeber*, edd. Kemp Malone and Martin B. Ruud (Minneapolis, 1929), pp. 14–20.

[2] Compare the reverse formations, with identical meanings, below in 4 (*b*). Compound elements are shifted easily, as one would expect in formulaic alliterative verse.

[3] The first element means *strong*. Hence the compound adjective can be translated only according to its poetic context; used of a victorious hero it will mean *stout-hearted*, of a respected ruler *magnanimous*, of a tyrant *fiercely arrogant*, of drunken warriors *violent in spirit*.

(*b*) Adverb + noun = adjective: blíðe-mód *cheerful,* éaþ-mód *humble,* ofer-mód *proud.*

B. Verbal Compounding with Prefixes[4]

á- (1) Gives intensive (especially with verbs of motion), perfective, or privative force: beran *carry,* á-beran *carry away;* drífan *drive,* á-drífan *drive out;* libban *live,* á-libban *survive;* sendan *send,* á-sendan *dispatch;* sœ́ćan *seek,* á-sœ́ćan *seek out.*

(2) With no apparent function: bídan *await,* á-bídan *await;* fyllan *fill, fulfill,* á-fyllan *fill, fulfill.*

be- (1) Intensive or perfective, often expressing result of, or response to, the action of the verb-stem: bycgan *buy,* be-bycgan *sell;* cuman *come,* be-cuman *become, happen;* singan *sing,* be-singan *bewail.*

(2) Makes intransitive verbs transitive: scéawian *look,* be-scéawian *watch;* sorgian *care,* be-sorgian *care for;* wœ́pan *weep,* be-wœ́pan *bewail.*

(3) Privative: ćeorfan *cut,* be-ćeorfan *cut off;* dǽlan *separate,* be-dǽlan *deprive.*

(4) With the sense "around, near, over": bugan *bend,* be-bugan *surround;* weorpan *throw,* be-weorpan *cover, surround;* witan *know,* be-witan *superintend.*

for- Intensive, perfective, often with destructive sense: brecan *break,* for-brecan *destroy;* ȝiefan *give,* for-ȝiefan *grant, forgive;* weorðan *become,* for-weorðan *perish.*

ȝe- (1) Perfective result or completion (as regularly in the past participle): ascian *ask,* ȝe-ascian *learn;* faran *go,* ȝe-faran *attain;* hléapan *leap,* ȝe-hléapan *mount;* winnan *strive,* ȝe-winnan *conquer.*

(2) Makes intransitive verbs transitive: friȝnan *ask,* ȝe-friȝnan *learn by asking;* rídan *ride,* ȝe-rídan *gain, reach by riding.*

(3) Without apparent function: ćéosan *choose,* ȝe-ćéosan *choose;* healdan *hold,* ȝe-healdan *hold;* secgan *say,* ȝe-secgan *say.*

of- Perfective and intensive: ȝiefan *give,* of-ȝiefan *give up, abandon;* sléan *strike,* of-sléan *strike down, kill.*

ofer- Adds sense of "over, above, beyond" in degree or quality: bídan *await,* ofer-bídan *outlast;* cuman *come,* ofer-cuman *overcome;* gán *go,* ofer-gán *overrun, traverse, pass away;* gangan *go,* ofer-gangan *conquer, transgress;* winnan *strive,* ofer-winnan *conquer.*

on- Inceptive (connotes the beginning of an action) or reversive: cweðan *say,* on-cweðan *respond;* wríon *cover,* on-wríon *uncover, reveal;* ǽlan *burn,* on-ǽlan *kindle.*

oþ- (1) Expresses concepts of "at, toward, beside": clífan *stick,* oþ-clífan *cleave to;* standan *stand,* oþ-standan *baffle;* wítan *blame,* oþ-wítan *reproach.*

(2) Expresses concepts of "away, forth": beran *carry,* oþ-beran *carry away;* fléogan *fly,* oþ-fléogan *fly away.*

[4]Verbal suffixes in the poetry are comparatively rare and are fully glossed in the dictionary.

to- Perfective, intensive, often destructive: berstan *burst*, to-berstan *burst asunder*; drífan *drive*, to-drífan *disperse*; dǽlan *divide*, to-dǽlan *scatter*; weorpan *throw*, to-weorpan *throw down, destroy*.

wiþ- Expresses concepts of "against, away": faran *go*, wiþ-faran *escape*; sacan *fight*, wiþ-sacan *oppose, refuse*; standan *stand*, wiþ-standan *oppose, withstand*.

ymb- Expresses concepts of "around, about": fón *take*, ymb-fón *grasp, clasp, surround*; sittan *sit down*, ymb-sittan *surround, reflect upon*.

þurh- Expresses concepts of "through, thorough(ly)": brecan *break*, þurh-brecan *break through*; drífan *drive*, þurh-drífan *pierce, permeate*; téon *draw, lead*, þurh-téon *accomplish*.

C. Compounding of Nouns, Adjectives, Adverbs, and Prepositions with Affixes

I. PREFIXES

á- (1) With nouns and adjectives derived from perfective or intensive verbs: á-líesan *release*, á-líesing *redemption*; á-rǽdan *determine*, á-rǽd *determined, fixed*.

(2) (Also ǽȝ-): Generalizes stem-meanings of pronouns and adverbs: á-hwæðer *someone, each, either of two*; á-hwǽr *anywhere*; á-wiht *aught, anything*.

an- Weakened form of *and-* (see below) expressing concepts of "opposite, against, toward, in reply to": an-bid *expectation*; an-feng *seizing, attack*; an-líć-ness *likeness*.

and- (See above): and-ȝiet *understanding*; and-léan *recompense*; and-rysnu *propriety*; and-saca *opponent*; and-wlita *face, appearance*.

be- (Unstressed): Forms substantives from verbs, and to these and other words often adds the sense of "at, by, near, around": be-bod *command*; be-foran *before*; be-gang *circuit*; be-hindan *behind*; be-útan *without, outside*.

bí- (Stressed; as above): bí-genȝa *inhabitant, cultivator*; bí-spell *parable, proverb*.

for- With nouns derived from intensive or perfective verbs; with adjectives and adverbs as intensive and pejorative: for-ȝief-ness *forgiveness*; for-hogodness *contempt*; for-maniȝ *very many*; for-wel *exceedingly*; for-cúþ *infamous*.

fore- Expresses concepts of priority and superiority: fore-genȝa *fore-runner, ancestor*; fore-mihtiȝ *very mighty*; fore-mǽre *pre-eminent*; fore-þanc *forethought, providence*.

ȝe- (1) Association, perfective result, completion of action: ȝe-bróðor *brothers*; ȝe-frǽȝe *renowned*; ȝe-fćra *companion in travel*; ȝe-líć *similar*; ȝe-mót *meeting*; ȝe-sibb *related*; ȝe-stréon *collected wealth, treasure*; ȝe-sund *sound, safe*.

(2) Without apparent function: ȝe-féa *joy*; ȝe-hlynn *noise*; ȝe-reord *speech*; ȝe-þyldiȝ *patient*.

inn- Expresses concepts of "in, into"; also intensive: inn-dryhten *nobly distinguished*; inn-flćde *full of water, overflowing*; inn-fród *very old, wise*; inn-gang *entrance*; inn-lende *native*; inn-weard *within*.

ofer- Expresses concepts of superiority or excess: ofer-ćeald *very cold*; ofer-ȝiet-ness *forgetfulness*; ofer-mód *pride*; ofer-mæȝen *overwhelming force*; ofer-wealdend *supreme ruler.*

un- (1) Negative and pejorative: un-bealu *innocence*; un-cúþ *unknown*; un-fæȝer *hideous*; un-ȝéara *lately*; un-grund *bottomless*; un-rǽd *bad counsel*; un-tréowþ *bad faith*; un-þanc *displeasure.*

    (2) Intensive (rare and problematical): un-forht *very frightenened*; un-gléaw *very sharp*; un-hár *very grey.*

upp- Expresses concepts of "up, away from": upp-cyme *rising*; up-heofon *high heaven*; upp-lang *upright*; upp-stiȝe *ascension*; upp-weard *upward.*

út- Expresses concepts of "out, away": út-fús *eager to set out*; út-gang *exit*; út-gár-secg *furthest ocean*; út-síþ *departure.*

ymb- Expresses concepts of "about, around": ymb-hoga *anxiety*; ymb-hwyrft *circuit*; ymb-sittend *neighbor*; ymb-útan *round about.*

æf- Separative, intensive, perfective: æf-lást *a wandering from the course*; æf-þanca *grudge*; æf-ćést *malice.*

æfter- "After" with a sense of continuation or response: æfter-léan *recompense*; æfter-weard *following.*

II. SUFFIXES

-dóm Connotes "power, quality, condition of" the stem, thus forming abstractions from other nouns and adjectives: cáser-dóm *empire*; cyne-dóm *kingdom*; frío-dóm *freedom*; wís-dóm *wisdom.*

-end Present participial ending used to form masculine nouns of agency: Dœmend *Judge*; Hǽlend *Saviour*; Scieppend *Creator*; wíȝend *fighter*; weoruld-búend *world-dweller, human being.*

-ere Forms masculine nouns of agency from other nouns and verbs: bócere *scribe, scholar*; sangere *singer.*

-full "Full, full of, characterized by," added to other adjectives and to abstract nouns: forht-full *timid*; ȝe-léaf-full *pious*; ȝeorn-full *eager*; sorg-full *sad*; weorþ-full *illustrious.*

-fæst "Firm in, fixed in" the quality of the stem: ár-fæst *honorable*; sóþ-fæst *righteous.*

-iȝ Connotes "having the qualities of, full of"; used to form adjectives from nouns: blódiȝ *bloody*; dyrstiȝ *daring*; háliȝ *holy*; sáriȝ *sad*; wittiȝ *wise.*

-ing (1) "Son of, proceeding from or descending from, associated with": æðeling *son of a noble, prince*; brenting *creature of the high sea, ship*; ierming *wretch.*

    (2) Forms abstract feminine nouns from weak verbs of class I: mœting *meeting*; nœðing *audacity*; wending *change, turning.*

-lang Connotes "belonging to, dependent on": dæȝ-lang *day-long*; ealdor-lang *life-long*; upp-lang *upright.*

-léas "Lacking, without": forms adjectives from nouns: dréam-léas *joyless*; ende-léas *endless*; grund-léas *bottomless*; sorg-léas *happy.*

-líć Connotes "form or quality of" the noun or adjective from which a new adjective is formed: cyne-líć *regal*; ȝe-sewen-líć *visible*; swíþ-líć *very great.*

-líće Adverbial; based on the above: éaþ-mód-líće *humbly*; glæd-líće *happily*; sóþ-líće *truly*.

-ness Connotes "state or condition of"; forms abstract feminine nouns from adjectives: gód-ness *goodness*; ídel-ness *frivolity*; mennisc-ness *humanity*; riht-wís-ness *righteousness*; ǽ-fæst-ness *piety*.

-sciepe Connotes "state or condition of, skill or function of"; forms abstract masculine nouns: bod-sciepe *message, embassy*; dryht-sciepe *rulership*; féond-sciepe *enmity*; mæȝen-sciepe *power*; weorþ-sciepe *honor, dignity*.

-ung Forms abstract feminine nouns from weak verbs of class II: blœ́dsung *blessing*; costnung *temptation*; héofung *lamentation*; weorðung *honor*.

On Arrangement and Abbreviations

A. Listed *vs.* Unlisted Forms

The head-words listed are the shortest forms appearing in the poetry from which related (compounded) forms can be inferred. Transparent compounds are omitted, as are forms with affixes (most commonly the prefix ȝe-) that do not modify the meaning of the stems, or that modify them in regular and transparent ways, unless these forms appear in the poetry only with such affixes. Examples are:

LISTED	UNLISTED
eald *old*; sweord *sword*	eald-sweord *ancient sword*
stán *stone*; clif *cliff*	stán-clif *rocky cliff*
bod *command*	ȝe-bod *command*
ȝe-þrang *throng*	þrang *throng* [does not appear as a simplex]
meltan *melt*	ȝe-meltan *melt away*
open *open*; openian *to open*	ȝe-openian *to open*; open-líċe *openly*
brecan *break*, etc.	á-, be-, for-, ȝe-, to-, þurh-brecan [with meanings implicit in the simplex stem, as fully listed in the dictionary, and transparent from the prefixed forms]
standan *stand*; á-, be-, for-, ȝe-, of-, oþ-, wiþ-, ymb-, æt-standan [with distinctive, not always transparent meanings]	

B. Grammatical Identifications

1. NOUNS. Nominative singular forms, with variants, are given alone when plurals do not appear in the poetry; nominative-accusative plural forms are given in parentheses: lamb(or) (lambru) *n.* lamb = the neuter noun, lamb/lambor *lamb* appears with nominative-accusative plural, lambru *lambs*.

2. ADJECTIVES AND ADVERBS. Irregular compared forms are given in parentheses: gód (betera, betst) *aj.* good, better, best.

3. VERBS. Principal parts (with variants, and abbreviated when possible) of strong (vocalic), anomalous, and class I weak (consonantal) verbs (when the latter show a vowel different from that of the present system) are given in parentheses. Strong verbs are to be expanded from their gradation vowels thus: bídan (á, i, i) *1* wait = bídan, bád, bidon, -biden; ćéosan (éa, curon, o) *2* choose = ćéosan, ćéas, curon, -coren. Uncontracted infinitive forms, often metrically significant, are given in brackets: séon [<*seohwan, <*sehwan]. As principal parts of preterite-present verbs are listed the infinitive, first and second person singular present

indicative, first person singular preterite indicative: witan (wát, wást, wisse/wiste) *prp.* know.

C. Pronunciation and Special Symbols

1. The acute accent distinguishes long vowels from short: ac *but*, ác *oak*; col *coal*, cól *cool*; full *full*, fúl *foul*.

2. The same mark distinguishes palatal ´ from velar *c* [k]: cræft *skill*, cú *cow*, rinc *man*, drincan *drink*; ćéosan *choose*, ćiecen *chicken*, ćiriće *church*, benć *bench*, streććan *stretch*, drenćan *"drench," cause to drink*.

3. The same mark distinguishes palatal [nǵ] from velar [ng]: cyning *king*, finger *finger*, strengþ *strength*; fenǵ *grasp*, henǵest *horse*, senǵan *singe*.

4. Not marked with a palatal diacritic, because always palatal except after a back vowel, is the consonant group [cg]: brycg *bridge*, ecg *edge*, licgan *lie*, secgan *say*; mucg-wyrt *mugwort*.

5. Not marked with a platal diacritic is the consonant group [sc], which is most frequently palatal, i.e. always initially (scip *ship*, scort *short*, scúr *shower*, scrúd *"shroud," garment*, scæft *shaft*), internally before front vowels (fisces *fish's*, wasceþ *washes*), internally after mutated vowels (hyscan *deride*, wýscan *wish*), and finally after front vowels (disc *dish*, Englisc *English*, fisc *fish*); biscop *bishop*, with the palatal pronunciation of the Modern English word, is irregular. The consonant group is pronounced [sk] only internally before back vowels (ascaþ *asks*, and thus in the infinitive, ascian *ask*; basilisca *basilisk*, discas *dishes*, fiscas *fishes*) unless the preceding vowel is mutated (hyscan *deride*, wýscan *wish*), and finally after back vowels (husc *scorn*, túsc *tusk*).

6. The velar stop and spirant *g* and "yogh," the palatal spirant [ʒ], are distinguished by these two symbols, although in the writing of Old English only the latter was used: glæd *glad*, gold *gold*, guma *man*, burg *stronghold*, nigun *nine*, boga *bow*, dagas *days*; ʒéar *year*, ʒeong *young*, ʒíet *yet*, fæʒer *fair*, seʒl *sail*, háliʒ *holy*, dæʒ *day*.

7. "Thorn," the voiceless spirant [þ], usually initial or final, and "eth," the voiced spirant [ð], always internal, are distinguished by these two symbols, although in the Old English period voiced and unvoiced sounds were represented by both: þing *thing*, þúsend *thousand*, siþþan *after*, áþ *oath*, norþ *north*, eorþ-líć *earthly*; eorðe *earth*, áðas *oaths*, norðan *from the north*.

D. Frequency Numbers

For single words, Arabic numbers in parentheses refer to the unit number in *A Grouped Frequency Word-List* (see above, pp. v–vi). For compounds, they refer to the unit number of the second (or the last significant) element; in the case of rare or unique compounds they may refer to total frequencies. Appropriate numbers are supplied for words omitted from the *Word-List*. When required by such additions, or when related words were separated in the *Word-List*, frequency units are re-grouped and renumbered here. In a few cases, therefore, numbers appear in the dictionary which are true guides to poetic frequencies but blind guides to the present edition of the *Word-List*.

E. Alphabetization

Both initially and internally, the special symbols [þ], [æ], and [œ], in that order, follow the end of the Latin alphabet. [ð] follows the ordinary *d*. *G* and [ʒ] are alphabetized together. Thus the order of a hypothetical sequence might be: zefferus, þá, þeʒn, þegu, þridian, þriðing, þý, þæt, þœlian. The prefix ʒe- is disregarded initially (ʒe-scæft follows scæft) but alphabetized like -ge- internally. Verbal prefixes (á, be-, for-, etc.) are also disregarded in the alphabetization, but non-verbal forms with prefixes will be found under the initial letter of the prefix. The reader should therefore look under the first letter of the stem for compounded verbs, but under the first letter of the complete form for all other words. The symbol ∼ indicates the preceding head-word repeated: ár (∼as) = ár (áras); gúþ, ∼mód = gúþ, gúþ-mód; standan, á∼ = standan, á-standan.

F. Abbreviations

acc. accusative
aj. adjective
anv. anomalous verb
aor. aorist
art. article
av. adverb(ial)
cj. conjunction
comp. comparative
constr. construction
correl. correlative
cp. compare
dat. dative
def. defective
f. feminine noun
g. genitive
imp. impersonal
ind. indicative
indecl. indeclinable

instr. instrumental
intens. intensive
interrog. interrogative
intr. intransitive
irreg. irregular
Lat. Latin
m. masculine noun
n. neuter noun
num. number
pass. passive
pers. person(al)
pl. plural
poss. possessive
ppl. participle, participial
pref. prefix
prep. preposition
pres. present
pret. preterite

prop. proper
prp. preterite-present verb
rel. relative
sb. substantive
sg. singular
superl. superlative
suff. suffix
tr. transitive
vb., vbl. verb(al)
I-III weak verb classes
1-7 strong verb classes
see (in cross-references)
    often means "see also"
*** = pre-literary form
< = "changed from"
(?) = doubtful form or
    meaning

Contents

A SHORT DICTIONARY OF
ANGLO-SAXON POETRY

A

á *av.* always, ever (377)

á- *pref.* (*intensive, perfective, privative with vbs., vbl. prefixes*) (1354)

∼hafen-ness (∼a) *f.* elevation (771)

∼líes-ness *f.sg.* redemption (224)

∼marod *ppl.aj.* confused, perplexed (1)

∼níehst *av.* last (120)

∼rǽd *aj.* determined, fixed (174)

∼wierȝda (∼n) *m.* devil, fiend (56)

∼wierȝed *ppl.aj.* damned; malignant (56)

∼wiht, -wuht *n.sg.* aught, anything, something: *av.* at all (245)

abal *see* afol

abbud (∼as) *m.* abbot (1)

ac *cj.* on the contrary, but; and yet; and; (*interrog. particle*) and indeed (459)

ác (ǽć) *f.* oak-tree; ship of oak; name of long A-rune (*irreg.pl.* ∼as) (7)

acan (ó, ó, a) *6* ache, hurt (2)

ȝe-áclian *II* frighten (13)

ácol *aj.* frightened (13)

ád (∼as) *m.* fire; pyre (32)

∼lama (?) (∼n) *m.* one crippled by fire (?) (6)

adel(a) *m.sg.* dirt, dirty place (1)

adesa (∼n) *m.* adz, hatchet (1)

ádl (∼a) *f.* illness, infirmity (23)

áðol-ware *m.pl.* citizens (?) (1)

áðum (∼as) *m.* son-in-law (2)

∼swéoras *m.pl.* son-in-law and father-in-law (3)

afol/abal *n.sg.* power, might (1)

áfor *aj.* bitter, fierce (2)

ág- *pref.* fearful, fearsome (218)

∼lǽć (∼) *n.* calamity, terror (218)

∼lǽća (∼n) *m.* terrible enemy; monster; hero (218)

ágan (áh, áhst, áhte) *prp.* possess, have, rule (370)

ágen *aj.* (one's) own (370)

ágend (∼) *m.* owner, ruler: ∼e *ppl.aj.* owning, possessing (370)

ágnian/ǽgnian *II* appropriate to oneself (370)

agof [<agob] *reversed spelling for* boga *m.* bow (172)

áh *see* ágan

alan (ó, ó, a) *6* grow (1)

alor (alras) *m.* alder-tree (1)

ám (∼as) *m.* read or slay of a loom (2)

amber *m.f.n.* pail, pitcher (1)

ambiht (∼as) *m.* messenger, officer (19)

ambiht (∼u) *n.* office, function (19)

an-, on- *pref.* against, opposite, parallel to, towards, in reply to (*weakened forms of* and-, *signifying inception, intensification, antithesis*) (294)

∼bid *n.sg.* expectation, waiting (150)

∼cýðiȝ *aj.* knowing, revealing (539)

∼cýþþ *f.sg.* pain, horror (539)

∼fenȝ (∼as) *m.* seizing, attack (198)

∼floga *m.sg.* attacking flier (123)

∼ȝe-trum *n.sg.* host, troop, body of men (82)

∼ȝinn *n.sg.* beginning, attack, undertaking (236)

∼gris-líć *aj.* fearful, grisly (1)

∼hár (?) *aj.* very grey (26)

∼hoga (∼n) *m.* anxiety, trouble (571)

∼hyȝdiȝ *aj.* strong-minded, stubborn (571)

∼líć, -e *aj.av.* similar(ly) (322)

∼líć-ness (∼a) *f.* image, likeness; parable (322)

∼mœ́dla (∼n) *m.* pride, pomp, arrogance (840)

3

∼rǽd *aj.* resolute; determined (174)

∼síen (∼a) *f.* face, form; aspect; sight (494)

∼síene *aj.* visible (494)

∼weald *m.sg.* power, rule, command: *aj.* powerful (526)

∼wealda *m.sg.* lord, ruler (526)

án *num.pron.aj.* one, the one, a single one, a certain one; only, unique (850)

∼dǽȝe *aj.* lasting a day (502)

∼floga *m.sg.* solitary flier (123)

∼haga (∼n) *m.* solitary dweller (22)

∼líepe *aj.* solitary, alone (15)

∼mód *aj.* bold, resolute; unanimous (840)

∼mœde *n.sg.* unanimity (840)

∼pæþ (-paðas) *m.* narrow path; lonely way (17)

∼rǽd *aj.* resolute (174)

∼stapa (∼n) *m.* a solitary, one who goes about alone (39)

∼tíd *f.sg.* due time, appointed hour (194)

ána *wk.aj.* alone (850)

ánad *n.sg.* desert, solitude (850)

ancor (∼as) *m.* anchor (6)

and *cj.* and; if (5001)

and- *pref.* against, opposite, parallel to, towards, in reply to, corresponding to; *cp.* an-, on- (294)

∼cwiss (∼a) *f.* reply (430)

∼fenȝ *m.sg.* receiver; defender (?) (198)

∼fenȝa (∼n) *m.* receiver; defender (198)

∼fenȝe *aj.* receptive (198)

∼ȝiet *n.sg.* understanding, intelligence (166)

∼ȝiete *aj.* manifest (166)

∼lang *aj.* continuous, entire; related (?); at the side (of someone in battle) (?) (286)

∼lifa (∼n) *m.* food, sustenance (600)

∼lifen (∼a) *f.* food, sustenance (600)

∼risnum *av.dat.* courteously, with propriety (17)

∼saca (∼n) *m.* adversary (466)

∼swaru *f.sg.* answer (96)

∼weard *aj.* present, opposite (882)

∼weorc (∼) *n.* matter, substance; cause (538)

∼wís *aj.* skilled (764)

∼wist *f.sg.* support; station (4189)

∼wlita (∼n) *m.* face, appearance (218)

∼wyrde *n.sg.* answer (631)

anda *m.sg.* vexation, anger (15)

andet-ness (∼a) *f.* confession, acknowledgment (56)

andettan *I* acknowledge, confess, promise (56)

anga (∼n) *m.* point, head (of arrow) (1)

ánga *wk.aj.* sole, only (850)

Angel-Seaxe *m.pl.* the Anglo-Saxons, the English (11)

Angle *m.pl.* the English (11)

ang-ness (∼a) *f.* anxiety, sorrow (16)

ann *see* unnan

ánunga *av.* completely, altogether (850)

apostol (∼as) *m.* apostle (4)

ár (∼as) *m.* messenger (31)

ár (∼a) *f.* honor; benefit, grace, favor; estate, property (172)

∼fæst *aj.* honorable; distinguished; gracious; pious; merciful (372)

∼stæf (-stafas) *m.* kindness, favor, grace (40)

∼wesa (∼n) *m.* honored one; lord: *aj.* honored (4189)

ár (∼a) *f.* oar (6)

áre (áran) *f.* honor; benefit, grace, favor; mercy; virtue (172)

árian *II* honor, respect; pity, be merciful to; glorify (172)

arod *aj.* swift, bold (2)

árum *av.dat.* honorably (172)

áscian *II* ask, seek, inquire, demand: ȝe∼ find out, hear; learn (16)

áscung (∼a) *f.* inquiry (16)

aspide (aspidas) *m.* asp (3)

assa (∼n) *m.* ass (1)

atol (∼) *n.* evil, terror, horror: *aj.* evil, terrible, loathsome (50)

átor (átru) *n.* poison (55)

~láðe *f.sg.* betony, *Betonica officinalis* (197)

~tán (~as) *m.* deadly twiglike etching (?) (17)

áwa *av.* always, ever (377)

áþ (áðas) *m.* oath (23)

B

bá *see* bœ́ȝen

bád *f.sg.* forced contribution, levy (15)

bád *see* bídan

baðian *II* bathe (25)

ban- *pref.* deadly (111)

bán (~) *n.* bone (67)

~fág *aj.* decorated with bone (antlers?) (42)

~fæt (~fatu) *n.* "bone-vessel," body (31)

~helm *n.sg.* body-protector, shield (?); horn-decorated helmet (?) (164)

~hring (~as) *m.* vertebra (65)

~loca (~n) *m.* body; muscle (117)

bana (~n) *m.* slayer; death; the Devil (111)

band *see* bindan

bann (~) *n.* proclamation, command (15)

bannan (éo, éo, a) ⁊ proclaim; summon (15)

basilisca (~n) *m.* basilisk (1)

básnian *II* wait for (4)

basu *aj.* purple (2)

bát (~as) *m.* boat (17)

bát *see* bítan

be/bí *prep.* by, beside, at, with, about; of, concerning; for, through, according to (192)

be-, bí- *pref.* by, at, near, around (*also qualifies vbs., vbl. derivatives as intensive, perfective, privative*) (192)

~bod (~u) *n.* command, order; Commandment (209)

~foran *av.prep.* before (223)

~gang (~as) *m.* circuit; way; expanse (?) (264)

~hindan *av.prep.* behind (30)

~hœ́fe *aj.* useful, fitting (5)

~lifd *ppl.aj.* deprived of life, dead (600)

~twéon, -twéonum, -tweox, be . . . twéonum *prep.* between (34)

~útan *prep.* outside, without (231)

~waden *ppl.aj.* issued out of (52)

béacen (~) *n.* sign, symbol, token (52)

béacnian *II* make a sign, betoken (52)

béad *see* béodan

beadu *f.sg.* battle (54)

~léoma (~n) *m.* battle-light; flashing sword (49)

~rún *f.sg.* hostile speech (?); secret enmity (?) (78)

béag (~as) *m.* ring; *pl.* rings, jewelry, valuables (172)

béag *see* búgan

bealcettan *I* belch (4)

beald *aj.av.* bold, brave, confident; boldly, immediately (89)

bealdian *II* show oneself bold, be bold (89)

bealdor *m.sg.* bold man, chieftain (89)

bealg *see* belgan

bealu (~) *n.* evil, harm: *aj.* evil, pernicious (94)

béam (~as) *m.* piece of wood; tree; pillar; the Cross (130)

beard (~as) *m.* beard (1)

bearg (~as) *m.* swine, boar (1)

bearg *see* beorgan

bearhtm/breahtm (~as) *m.* brightness, flash; noise (27)

bearm (~as) *m.* bosom, lap; waist (of a ship); possession (19)

bearn (~) *m.* child, son (652)

bearn *see* biornan

bearu (bearwas) *m.* grove, copse (32)

béatan (éo, éo, éa) ⁊ strike, beat (12)

becc *m.sg.* brook, stream (1)

ȝe-bed (~u) *n.* prayer (150)

bedd (~) *n.* bed, couch; resting-place; grave (33)

5

bedd (~u) *n.* table, altar (7)

ʒe-bedda (~n) *m.f.* bedfellow; consort (33)

beden *see* biddan

beðung (~a) *f.* bathing; cataplasm, poultice (25)

belgan (ea, u, o) *3* be or grow angry (36)

bellan (beal, bullon, o) *3* bellow, roar (1)

benć (~a) *f.* bench (20)

bend (~as; ~a) *m.f.* bond, fetter; rope (135)

bendan *I* bend (135)

benn (~a) *f.* wound (111)

bennian *II* wound (111)

béod (~as) *m.* table (3)

béodan (éa, u, o) *2* offer, show; announce; command (209)

béoháta/bíota *m.sg.* challenger, champion, commander; boaster (?) (27)

béonn *see* bannan

béor *n.sg.* beer (18)

beorc *f.sg.* birch-tree; name of B-rune (1)

beorcan (ea, u, o) *3* bark (of a dog) (2)

beorðor *n.sg.* birth; child (652)

beorg (~as) *m.* hill, tumulus, barrow (398)

beorg (~e) *f.* protection, defense (398)

ʒe-beorg *n.sg.* defense, protection; refuge (398)

beorgan (ea, u, o) *3* conceal; protect, save, spare: be~ beware of, guard oneself against (398)

beorht (~) *n.* splendor (242)

beorht, ~e *aj.av.* bright(ly), clear(ly), beautiful(ly), glorious(ly) (242)

beorhtian *II* shine, sound out; sound clearly (242)

beorma (~n) *m.* yeast, brewer's barm (2)

beorn (~as) *m.* warrior, man (137)

béot *see* béatan

bera (~n) *m.* bear (animal) (2)

beran (æ, ǽ, o) *4* bear, carry, bring; wear; proceed: á~ bear, suffer; remove: for~ bear with, forbear; re-

strain: ʒe~ bring forth, produce: on~ impair, diminish, destroy: oþ~ carry away: to~ scatter: ymb~ surround: æt~ carry to; carry away (652)

bere (beran) *f.* covering (652)

berend (~) *m.* bearer: ~e *ppl.suff.* -bearing (652)

berian *I* make bare; clear away (8)

berie (beriʒan) *f.* berry (1)

berstan (æ, u, o) *3* burst, break, crack; crash; fall (23)

bet *av.* better (101)

~lić *aj.* splendid (101)

betera *aj.* better (101)

betst *aj.av.* best (101)

bí *see* be

bí- *pref.* by, at, near, around: *cp.* be- (192)

~genʒa (~n) *m.* cultivator, inhabitant (264)

~rihte *prep.* next to, adjoining (417)

~spell (~) *n.* parable (66)

~sæćć *f.sg.* approach (466)

bid *n.sg.* delay, halt (160)

~fæst *aj.* firm, stationary (372)

bídan (á, i, i) *1* wait, await; endure, experience; delay, remain: á~ await: ʒe~ (*intr.*) await, live to experience: ofer~ outlast, outlive: on~ await (160)

biddan (bæd, ǽ, e) *1-5* ask, order; (*refl.*) pray (150)

bíding (~a) *f.* abode, biding place (160)

bíecnan *I* make a sign, betoken (52)

bíecning (~a) *f.* indication (52)

bíecþ (~a) *f.* token, sign (52)

bíeʒan *I* cause to bend; blunt, turn back; crush, humiliate (172)

bielć *m.sg.* pride (4)

bielćan *I* belch, utter, pour out (4)

bielćed-swíera *aj.* swollen-necked (1)

bieldan *I* embolden, encourage, excite (89)

bieldu (~) *f.* boldness, firmness (89)

bíeme (bíeman) *f.* trumpet (of wood) (130)

bierʒan *I* taste, eat (13)

bierhtan *I* brighten (242)

bierhtu (∼) *f.* brightness (242)

bierman *I* ferment, swell; be proud (2)

bíewan *I* polish, prepare, cleanse (2)

bíewend (∼) *m.* polisher (2)

bîfian *II* tremble; quake (of the earth) (24)

bilewit *aj.* pure, innocent (14)

bill (∼) *n.* sword (36)

ʒe-bind (∼) *n.* bond, fetter; constraint; expanse (135)

bindan (a, u, u) *3* bind, tie up; freeze solid (135)

bindere (∼as) *m.* one who binds (135)

binn (∼a) *f.* manger (1)

binnan *prep.* within (4747)

bío (∼n) *f.* bee; *first element in pers. name* Bío-wulf (Béo-wulf) (60)

∼bréad *n.sg.* "bee-bread," honey-comb (3)

bíon *consuetudinal pres. vb.* will be, be supposed to be, apt to be (4189)

biornan (ea, u, o) *3* burn (145)

bíot (∼) *n.* vow, promise; threat (27)

bíota *see* béoháta

bíotian *II* make a vow or pledge; boast, threaten (27)

bíotung (∼a) *f.* promise, vow (27)

biscop (∼as) *m.* bishop, (18)

bíses *m.sg.* bissextile, leap year; intercalary day (1)

bisgung *f.sg.* affliction (39)

bisiʒ *aj.* busy; troubled (39)

bisiʒian *II* occupy oneself; trouble, afflict (39)

bisigu (bisiga) *f.* business, preoccupation, trouble (39)

bismer *m.f.n.* scorn, mockery (18)

bismerian *II* scorn, mock (18)

bítan (á, i, i) *1* bite, cut, wound: on∼ taste, partake of (97)

bite (∼) *m.* bite, cut (97)

biter, ∼e *aj.av.* sharp(ly), cruel(ly) (97)

blác *aj.* bright, shining; pale, pallid, livid (56)

∼ern *n.sg.* lantern (18)

∼hléor *aj.* with shining cheeks (22)

blác *see* blícan

blácian *II* turn pale (56)

blanca (∼n) *m.* white horse (3)

bland *n.sg.* mingling, turbulence (21)

blandan (é, é, a) *7* mingle, mix (21)

blanden-feax *aj.* with greying hair (19)

blann *see* blinnan

blát *m.sg.* moan (2)

blát, ∼e *aj.av.* pale, pallidly; livid(ly) (5)

blátian *II* grow pale (5)

bláwan (éo, éo, á) *7* blow (of the wind) (9)

bléat, ∼e, *aj.av.* wretched(ly) (2)

bléaþ *aj.* gentle; shy, timid (2)

blenćan *I* deceive, cheat (1)

blénd *see* blandan

blendan *I* make blind, deceive (24)

bléot *see* blótan

bléow *see* blówan

blícan (á, i, i) *1* shine, glitter, sparkle (56)

blíð(e) *aj.* happy; gentle; quiet, calm (110)

blíðe *av.* happily; kindly; mildly (110)

blind *aj.* blind; dark; unintelligent (24)

blinn *n.sg.* cessation (11)

blinnan (a, u, u) *3* cease, stop (11)

blío-bryʒd (∼as) *m.* variegated color (60)

ʒe-blíod *aj.* beautiful (16)

blío(h) (∼) *n.* color; appearance (16)

bliss (∼a) *f.* bliss, joy, exultation; pleasure; kindness, grace (122)

blissian *II* rejoice, be glad; gladden, delight (122)

-blissiende *ppl.suff.* rejoicing (122)

blód (∼) *n.* blood (159)

∼ʒéota (∼n) *m.* bloodshed (42)

∼iʒ *aj.* bloody (159)

∼lifer (∼a) *f.* clotted blood (78)

blódiʒian *II* make bloody (159)

blóstm (∼as; ∼a) *m.f.* blossom, bloom (14)

blóstma (∼n) *m.* blossom, bloom (14)

blót (∼) *n.* sacrifice (30)

∼monaþ *m.sg.* November (30)

blótan (éo, éo, ó) *7* sacrifice (30)

blówan (éo, éo, ó) *7* bloom, flourish (26)

blunnon *see* blinnan

blyse *f.sg.* blaze (2)

blæc *aj.* dark, black (13)

blǽćan *I* bleach (56)

blæd (bladu) *n.* leaf (122)

blǽd (∼as) *m.* spirit; inspiration; glory, prosperity (122)

blǽd (∼a) *f.* foliage, fruit (122)

∼hwæt *aj.* copious, fruitful (47)

ʒe-blǽd-fæst *aj.* glorious (372)

blǽse (blǽsan) *f.* blaze, flame (2)

blǽst (∼as) *m.* flame, fire; blast (of wind) (5)

blǽtan *I* bleat (2)

blœ́dan *I* bleed (159)

blœ́dsian/blœ́tsian *II* bless; benefit (159)

blœ́dsung (∼a) *f.* blessing (159)

bóc (bœ́ć) *f.n.* book (64)

∼wudu (-wuda) *m.* beech-tree (90)

bócere (bóceras) *m.* writer, scribe, author, scholar (64)

bod (∼u) *n.* command; Commandment (209)

∼sciepe *m.sg.* command; message (340)

boda (∼n) *m.* messenger (209)

boden *see* béodan

bodian *II* announce, relate, preach (209)

bóg (∼as) *m.* shoulder, arm; back (of a horse); bough (3)

boga (∼n) *m.* bow (weapon); what is arched, bent, twisted (172)

bogen *see* búgan

bóian *II* boast (1)

bolca (∼n) *m.* gang-plank (3)

bold/botl (∼) *n.* building, hall, manor (38)

bolgen *see* belgan

bolla (∼n) *m.* bowl, cup (1)

bolster (bolstras) *m.* cushion (2)

bora (∼n) *m.* bearer; piercer (?) (652)

borcian (?) *II* bark (?) (2)

bord (∼) *n.* board, plank, shield, side of a ship; ship (73)

∼stæþ (-staðu) *n.* shore (172)

borde (bordan) *f.* board, table (73)

borg-sorg *f.sg.* "borrow-sorrow," lending-trouble (174)

boren *ppl.aj.* born, begotten (652)

boren *see* beran

ʒe-borga (∼n) *m.* protector (398)

borgen *see* beorgan

borian *II* place in a bored hole (1)

bornen *see* biornan

borsten *see* berstan

bósm (∼as) *m.* bosom, breast, lap; waist (of a ship); interior (20)

bót (∼a) *f.* remedy; atonement (101)

botl *see* bold

botm *m.sg.* bottom (4)

brád *n.sg.* expanse, sea (64)

brád (brǽdre/brádra, brádost) *aj.* broad, wide (64)

bráde *av.* far and wide (64)

bran *see* brinnan

brand (∼as) *m.* flame, burning wood; sword (20)

brant *aj.* towering (5)

brastl *m.sg.* crackling (2)

brastlian *II* crackle, roar (2)

bréac *see* brúcan

bréad *n.sg.* bread (3)

breahtm *see* bearhtm

bréat *see* bréotan

ʒe-brec *see* ʒe-bræc

brecan (æ, ǽ, o) *5-4* break, violate, destroy; break forth, burst through; press, urge, oppress (105)

brecþ (∼a) *f.* grief, heart-break (105)

brecþa (∼n) *m.* broken condition, sorrow (105)

bredian *II* restore, remake, transform (2)

bredian *II* cry out (1)

bredwian *II* strike down (2)

ʒe-bréfan *I* write down briefly (1)

ȝe-breȝd (~u) *n.* agitation, tossing (60)

breȝdan (bræȝd, brugdon, o) *3* move quickly, swing; unsheath; weave; change, be changed, vary: á~ draw, withdraw, swing, raise: for~ snatch away; transform: ȝe~ unsheath; draw breath; weave: ofer~ cover: on~ move quickly, start up; force open: oþ~ take away: to~ turn quickly, cast off (sleep); tear apart, divide; spread abroad (60)

bregu *m.sg.* lord, ruler (44)

brenȝan (bróhte) *I* bring, bring forth, lead (134)

brenting (~as) *m.* high-prowed ship (5)

a-bréoðan (éa, u, o) *2* fail, perish, come to grief (2)

bréost (~) *n.* chest, heart, breast (*commonly in pl.*) (107)

~toga *m.sg.* chieftain (95)

bréotan (éa, u, o) *2* break; slay (69)

brerd (~as) *m.* edge, surface (1)

bresne *see* bræsne

bridd (~as) *m.* young bird (3)

briȝd (~) *n.* change, play (of color) (60)

bri(ȝ)del(s) (~as) *m.* bridle (60)

brim (~u) *n.* sea (53)

bringan (*def.; ppl.* brungen) *3* bring, bring forth, lead (134)

on-brinnan (a, u, u) *3* kindle (145)

bróc (~as) *m.* stream, brook (2)

brocen *see* brecan, brúcan

broðen *see* bréoðan

bróðor (~; bróðru) *m.* brother (67)

bróga (~n) *m.* terror (33)

brogden *see* breȝdan

brogden-mǽl *aj.* marked with wavy patterns: *as sb.* a sword so marked (57)

bróg-þréa *m.sg.* terrible distress (45)

bróhte *see* brenȝan

brosnian *II* decay, perish, disintegrate (10)

brosnung (~a) *f.* corruption, decay (10)

broten *see* bréotan

brú (~a) *f.* eye-lash (1)

brúcan (éa, u, o) *2* use, enjoy (94)

brugdon *see* breȝdan

brún *aj.* bright, glistening; brown (?) (17)

brungen *see* bringan

bruton *see* bréotan

bryće *m.sg.* use, service (94)

bryće *aj.* fragile, fleeting (105)

brýće *aj.* useful (94)

brycg (~a) *f.* bridge, causeway (5)

brycg(i)an *I-II* make a bridge (5)

brýd (~e) *f.* bride, wife, woman (48)

bryðen *f.sg.* brew, drink (1)

ȝe-bryȝdan *I* terrify (60)

brýnan *I* make shiny, redden (?) (17)

bryne *m.sg.* burning, conflagration (145)

bryrdan *I* incite, inspire (19)

brýsan *I* crush, pound (1)

bryten *aj.* wide, spacious; powerful (69)

brytnian *II* divide up (69)

brytta (~n) *m.* distributor, dispenser (69)

bryttian *II* break up, distribute (69)

ȝe-bræc, -brec (~u) *n.* breaking, crash, noise (105)

bræc *see* brecan

brǽdan *I* spread out, spread abroad (64)

brǽdra *see* brád

brǽdu *f.sg.* breadth (64)

bræȝd (~as) *m.* brandishing, movement; artifice, trick, betrayal (60)

bræȝd *see* breȝdan

ȝe-bræȝd-stafas *m.pl.* literary arts (40)

bræȝen *n.sg.* brain (1)

brǽr (~as) *m.* briar (1)

bræsne/bresne *aj.* strong (3)

brǽw (~as) *m.* brow (2)

brœ́ć *f.pl.* breeches (1)

brœ́ȝan *I* terrify (33)

brœ́man *I* honor, celebrate (27)

brœ́me *av.* solemnly (27)

brœ́mel (~as) *m.* thorn, bramble (1)

9

brœme(n) *aj.* famous, illustrious (27)

bú (∼) *n.* dwelling, settlement (114)

bú *see* bœʒen

búan, búde *see* bú(i)an

budon *see* béodan

búend (∼) *m.* dweller: ∼e *ppl.suff.* -dwelling (114)

búgan (béag, bugon, o) *2* bend, bow; rest; turn, avoid, escape, retreat: be∼ avoid; surround, encompass (172)

bú(i)an/búwan (búde, bún) *7-III* cultivate, dwell, settle (114)

bulgon *see* belgan

bunden *ppl.aj.* bound (135)

∼heord *aj.* with hair bound up (1)

∼stefna *m.sg.* ship with bound (iron-worked or ornamented) prow (118)

bundon *see* bindan

bune (bunan) *f.* cup (5)

búr(∼)*n.*apartment,sleeping quarters(6)

burg (byriʒ) *f.* stronghold, fortress; manor-house; town, city (398)

∼ende *m.sg.* city boundary (154)

burgon *see* beorgan

burna/burne (burnan) *m.f.* brook (6)

burnon *see* biornan

burn-sele (∼) *m.* bath-house (142)

burston *see* berstan

bútan *cj.* unless, save that, except that, but; except if, if only; *prep.* out of, against, without, except (231)

búwan *see* bú(i)an

bycgan (bohte) *I* buy: be∼ sell (20)

byden (∼a) *f.* barrel, tub (1)

bydla *see* bylda

byht (∼) *m.* dwelling (114)

bylda/bydla (∼n) *m.* builder (38)

býled *aj.* swollen (1)

∼bréost *aj.* puff-breasted (107)

á-bylʒan *I* anger, offend (36)

-byrd *f.suff.* nature, order, rank (652)

ʒe-byrde *aj.* innate, natural (652)

byrd-sciepe *m.sg.* child-bearing (340)

ʒe-byrd(u) (∼a; ∼) *f.n.* birth, origin, lineage; nature, quality; fate (652)

byrðen (∼a) *f.* burden (5)

byre (∼; byras) *m.* son (652)

byre *m.sg.* happening, event; opportunity (652)

byrele (byrelas) *m.* cupbearer (5)

byrelian *II* pour (a drink) (5)

ʒe-byrʒa (∼n) *m.* protector (398)

byrʒan *I* bury, conceal (398)

byrʒen (byrʒna) *f.* grave, tomb (398)

byrʒend (∼as) *m.* burier, gravedigger (398)

ʒe-byrian *I* happen; suit (652)

byrne (byrnan) *f.* chain-mail corselet, byrnie (32)

byrne *f.sg.* stream, brook (6)

byrniʒ *aj.* burning, fiery (145)

byrst (∼as) *m.* harm, damage (23)

býsen (býsna) *f.* example; exemplar; command (12)

bytlian *II* build (38)

bæc (bacu) *n.* back (13)

∼ling *av.* backwards, behind (*only in phrase* on ∼) (13)

bæd *see* biddan

bǽdan *I* compel; urge, press (15)

bǽde-wǽʒe *n.sg.* drinking vessel (9)

bǽl *n.sg.* fire, flame, funeral pyre (30)

bælć (∼as) *m.* covering, canopy (1)

bær *aj.* bare, exposed (8)

bær *see* beran

bǽr *f.sg.* bier (652)

ʒe-bǽran *I* conduct oneself (652)

ʒe-bǽre (-bǽru) *n.* behavior (652)

-bǽre *aj.suff.* productive of (652)

bærnan *I* burn (145)

bærst *see* berstan

bǽtan *I* bridle, harness (97)

bæþ (baðu) *n.* bath (25)

bœʒen (bá, bú) *num.* both (93)

bœn (∼e) *f.* petition (32)

∼tíd (∼a) *f.* time of supplication, Rogation days (194)

bœna (∼n) *m.* petitioner, suppliant (32)

bœtan *I* improve; atone for (101)

bœtend (∼) *m.* restorer (101)

C

cáf, ~e *aj.av.* active(ly), bold(ly) (4)

calc *m.sg.* shoe, sandal; for *calic* "chalice" (?), name of K-rune: ~rand *aj.* horse-shoe edged, shod (of a horse) (1)

cálend (~as) *m.* month (3)

~cwide *m.sg.* number of months, tale of days (430)

calic (~as) *m.* chalice (1)

calla *m.sg.* herald (2)

calu *aj.* bald (1)

camp (~as) *m.* battle, fight (66)

~ræden (~a) *f.* contest, war (174)

camp (~) *n.* fetter, bond (1)

campian *II* fight for (66)

candel (~a) *f.* candle, light (16)

cann *see* cunnan

cantic (~as) *m.* canticle, chant (4)

car, carian, caru *see* ćear, etc.

carc-ærn *n.sg.* prison (20)

carr (~as) *m.* rock (2)

cásere (~áseras) *m.* emperor (*esp.* of the Eastern Empire) (16)

ćeafl (~as) *m.* jaw (4)

ćeafor (~as) *m.* chafer, beetle (2)

~tún (~as) *m.* entrance hall, court (53)

ćeald *n.sg.* cold: *aj.* cold; painful, evil (94)

ćealf (~ru *m.* calf (3)

ćeallian *II*) call, shout (2)

ćéap (~ as) *m.* business transaction; bargain; price (18)

~éadiʒ *aj.* rich in goods (241)

ćéapian *II* transact business, buy (18)

ćéapung (~a) *f.* business, negotiation (18)

ćear *aj.* anxious, sorrowful (75)

~iʒ *aj.* anxious (75)

ćearf *see* ćeorfan

ćearian *II* be anxious, suffer distress (75)

ćearu (ćeara) *f.* anxiety, distress (75)

ćéas *f.sg.* quarrel, strife (173)

ćéas *see* ćéosan

-ćéasiʒ *aj.suff.* -choosing, -selecting (173)

ćeaster (ćeastra) *f.* large town, city (51)

céder *m.f.n.* cedar (3)

cellod *aj.* concave (?); convex (?); having a boss, studded (?); leather-covered (?) (2)

cempa (~n) *m.* fighter, warrior (66)

ćén *m.sg.* pine torch; name of C-rune (4)

cennan *I* declare, prove; name (539)

cennan *I* beget, bear (young); (*intr.*) increase (?) (55)

ćéol (~as) *m.* ship (34)

ćeolas *m.pl.* cold winds (94)

ćeole (ćeolan) *f.* throat (1)

ćeorfan (ea, curfon, o) *3* cut (9)

ćeorl (~as) *m.* man, husbandman, common freeman; simple fellow (13)

ćeorran (ea, curron, o) *3* creak (1)

ćéosan (éa, curon, o) *2* choose, elect, select; accept (173)

ćéowan (éa, cuwon, o) *2* chew (4)

ćídan *I* rebuke, blame (1)

ćícen *n.sg.* chicken, chick (1)

ćieʒan *I* call, call out, name (41)

ćiele *m.sg.* coolness, chill (94)

ćiepa (~n) *m.* merchant (18)

ʒe-ćíepan *I* do business, trade (18)

ćierm (~as) *m.* noise (23)

ćierman *I* cry out, make a noise (23)

ćierr (~as) *m.* turn, change; tide (?); occasion, time (71)

ćierran *I* turn, change, go; convert (in faith) (71)

ćiest (~e) *f.* troop, squad (173)

ćiest *f.sg.* chest, ark (1)

ćild (~ru) *n.* child (17)

ćildisc *aj.* as or like a child (17)

ćínan (cán, ćinon, i) *1* gape (1)

for-ćinnan (-cann, u, u) *3* destroy (1)

ćinn-beorg (~a) *f.* chin-guard on helmet (1)

circul (~as) *m.* circle (1)

ćiriće (ćirićan) *f.* church (13)

ćíþ (ćíðas) *m.* seed, young shoot (5)

clamm (~as) *m.* grip, vise (36)

clang *see* clingan

cláwu/cléa (cláwa; cláwan) *f.* claw (2)

cláþ (cláðas) *m.* cloth, article of clothing, clothes (4)

be-clemman *I* chain, shut up (36)

cléofan (éa, u, o) *2* split, cleave (3)

clibbor *aj.* clinging, sticky (3)

clíewen *n.* ball, mass, heap (1)

clif (~u) *n.* cliff (22)

clifa (~n) *m.* cell, chamber (3)

clífan (á, i, i) *1* stick, adhere (3)

clifian *II* adhere (3)

clingan (a, u, u) *3* shrink: be~ bind: ȝe~ shrivel, shrink (down into) (5)

clipian *II* call out (61)

clofen *see* cléofan

clúd (~as) *m.* mass of rocks (1)

clufon *see* cléofan

clungen *see* clingan

clúse (clúsan) *f.* lock, bolt; enclosure (8)

clústor (clústru) *n.* lock, bolt; cell, enclosure (8)

clymmian *II* climb, mount (1)

clympre *m.sg.* lump of metal (1)

clynnan *I* clang, resound (1)

clyppan *I* embrace (8)

be-clýsan *I* close, shut (8)

clǽne *aj.av.* clean, pure, innocent; entirely, to the full (96)

clǽnsian *II* purify, cleanse (96)

cnáwan (éo, éo, á) *7* recognize, know, perceive (63)

cnearr (~as) *m.* ship (2)

cnéo (~; ~wu) *n.* knee; degree of kinship; generation (45)

~riss (~a) *f.* generation, race, family (45)

ȝe-cnéodan (éa, u, o) *2* enroll (1)

cnéow *see* cnáwan

cniht (~as) *m.* boy, young man (29)

ȝe-cnóden *ppl.aj.* enrolled (1)

cnoll (~as) *m.* hill, knoll (1)

cnósl *n.sg.* family, relatives (8)

cnossian *II* knock, pound (20)

cnyssan *I* strike, knock against (20)

ȝe-cnǽwe *aj.* evident, well-known (63)

cóc (~as) *m.* cook (2)

cócer-panne (~) *f.* cooking-pan (2)

cocor (~as) *m.* quiver (1)

coðe/coðu *f.sg.* sickness (2)

cofa (~n) *m.* chamber, interior; enclosed place (*e.g.* ark, breast, body) (27)

cohhettan *I* cough, clear the throat (1)

col (~u) *n.* coal, ember (3)

cól *aj.* cool (94)

cólian *II* become cool, cool off (94)

colla (~n) *m.* slaughter (?); terror (?) (1)

collen-ferhþ *aj.* brave, bold; elated (13)

cóm *see* cuman

cométa (~n) *m.* comet (1)

corðor (~) *n.* troop (27)

coren *see* ćéosan

ȝe-coren-ness (~a) *f.* choice (173)

corfen *see* ćeorfan

corn (~) *n.* grain, wheat; grain, particle (8)

cost *aj.* tried, proved, excellent (173)

costian *II* tempt, try, prove (173)

cost(n)ung (~a) *f.* temptation (173)

cowen *see* ćéowan

coþ-líće *av.* miserably (2)

crang *see* cringan

créad *see* crúdan

créopan (éa, u, o) *2* creep (2)

cribb *f.sg.* crib, manger (1)

cring *n.sg.* fall, downfall, slaughter (20)

cringan (a, u, u) *3* fall to the ground (in battle) (20)

cristalla (~n) *m.* crystal (1)

Crísten (~as) *m.* Christian (2)

crístnian *II* baptize (2)

ȝe-crod (~u) *n.* crowd, throng (5)

croda *m.sg.* crowd, throng (5)

cropen *see* créopan

crúdan (éa, u, o) *2* crowd, press (2)

crungon *see* cringan

crǽft (~as; ~a) *m.f.* power, strength; force, host; ability, art, skill; trick (223)

~iȝ *aj.* powerful, potent; skillful, cunning (223)

ȝe-cræftan *I* contrive (223)

cræftȝa (~n) *m.* workman (223)

cræt (cratu) *n.* cart (2)

cú (cý) *f.* cow (1)

cúðe *av.* clearly (539)

cúðe *see* cunnan

culfer/culfre (culfran) *f.* dove (5)

culpe (culpan) *f.* fault (1)

cuma (~n) *m.* comer, visitor, stranger (544)

cuman (ó, ó, u) *4* come, go: á~ come out: be~ come, come to; become, happen; for~ overcome, surpass; ofer'~ overcome (544)

cumbol/cumbor (~) *n.* battle-standard, banner, ensign (15)

-cund *aj.suff.* coming from (544)

cunnan (cann, cannst, cúðe) *prp.* know, know how to: on~ accuse (539)

cunnian *II* try, attempt, tempt, find out (23)

cunnung (~a) *f.* temptation (23)

curfon *see* ćeorfan

curon *see* ćéosan

curron *see* ćeorran

cúsc *aj.* chaste, virtuous (1)

cuwon *see* ćéowan

cúþ *aj.* known, familiar, customary; certain; well-known, renowned (539)

~líće *av.* openly, manifestly; familiarly, kindly (322)

cwacian *II* quake, tremble (5)

cwalu *f.sg.* killing, death, murder (101)

cwánian *II* lament (5)

cwániȝ *aj.* sorrowful (5)

cweććan (cweahte) *I* shake, brandish (5)

cweart-ærn *n.sg.* prison (20)

cwealm (~as) *m.* killing, death (101)

cweden *see* cweðan

cwedol *aj.* talkative, eloquent (430)

cweðan (cwæþ, cwǽdon, e) *5* say, speak: á~ speak out, declare; banish, reject: be~ speak; reproach: for~ rebuke:

ȝe~ say, speak; on~ speak to; answer, reply (430)

cweðend (~) *m.* speaker (430)

cwelan (æ, ǽ, o) *4* die (101)

cwellan (cwealde) *I* kill (101)

cwellere (cwelleras) *m.* murderer, executioner (101)

cwene *f.sg.* woman (51)

cwić/cwucu *aj.* alive, living (70)

cwician *II* bring to life, quicken (70)

cwiddian *II* speak (430)

cwide (~) *m.* utterance, saying (430)

cwíðan *I* bewail, lament (11)

cwield *m.f.n.* destruction, death (101)

cwielman *I* kill (101)

cwolen *see* cwelan

cwucu *see* cwić

cwǽdon *see* cweðan

cwæl *see* cwelan

cwæþ *see* cweðan

cwǿman *I* please; serve (25)

ȝe-cwǿme *aj.* pleasing, pleasant, fit (25)

cwǿn (~e) *f.* woman; wife; queen (51)

cýðan *I* make known, announce: á~ proclaim, prove: for~ rebuke, reprove: ȝe~ make known, proclaim, relate, show, reveal (539)

cýðiȝ *aj.* knowing, aware (539)

cyll (~a) *f.* leather bottle (1)

cyme (cymas) *m.* coming, arrival (544)

cýme *aj.* fair, lovely, glorious (14)

ȝe-cynd (~a) *f.* nature, origin (49)

cynde *aj.* natural, innate (49)

ȝe-cynd(e) (-cyndu) *n.* nature, manner: *aj.* innate, inherited (49)

cyne- *pref.* royal (591)

cyning (~as) *m.* king (591)

~Wuldor *n.sg.* Glory of Kings, God (424)

cynn (~) *n.* kind, quality, species; generation, race, people, family; etiquette, propriety: *aj.* proper, suitable (389)

cyn-ren *n.sg.* generation, kind (389)

cypera (~n) *m.* spawning salmon (1)

cyre (∼) *m.* choice (173)

cyrten *aj.* fair, beautiful (1)

cyspan *I* bind, fetter (1)

cyssan *I* kiss (4)

cyst (∼e) *f.* choice; the best of, the élite; excellence, virtue (173)

∼iȝ *aj.* choice, good (173)

cýta (∼n) *m.* kite, bird of prey (1)

cýþþ(u) (cýþþa) *f.* knowledge, familiarity; home, native land; kindred, neighbors (539)

cǽȝ(e) (cǽga; cǽgan) *f.* key (4)

á-cǿlan *I* cool off (94)

cǿne *aj.* keen, bold, fierce (31)

cǿnþu (∼a) *f.* boldness (31)

D

ȝe-dafen *aj.* suitable (36)

ȝe-dafenian *II* befit, suit (36)

dagian *II* become day, dawn (502)

ȝe-dál (∼) *n.* distribution, partition, separation (210)

daroþ (daroðas) *m.* spear, dart (12)

daru (dara) *f.* harm, misfortune (12)

déad *aj.* dead (184)

déaf *aj.* deaf (9)

déaf *see* dúfan

déag *see* dugan

déagan (éo, éo, déaȝen) *7* hide, hide oneself(?) (38)

déagol/déogol *aj.* concealed, dark (38)

dealf *see* delfan

deall *aj.* proud; famous (7)

dearninga/dearnunga *av.* secretly, privately; insidiously (50)

dearr *see* durran

déaw *m.sg.* dew (16)

∼iȝ *aj.* dewy (16)

déaþ (déaðas) *m.* death (184)

delfan (ea, u, o) *3* dig, dig out (7)

denn (∼) *n.* den, lair (8)

dennian *II* flow (?); be wet, slippery (?) (1)

denu (dena) *f.* valley (8)

déog *see* déagan

déogol *see* déagol

déop (∼) *n.* the deep, abyss; hollow passage (111)

déop, ∼e *aj.av.* deep(ly), profound(ly) (111)

déor (∼) *n.* wild animal: *aj.* bold; violent (102)

deorc, ∼e *aj.av.* gloomy, sad; dark(ly), obscure(ly) (41)

derian *II* harm, injure (12)

díacon (∼as) *m.* deacon (1)

díefan *I* dip, immerse (7)

ȝe-díegan *I* carry out; endure, survive, escape (182)

díeȝlan *I* hide (38)

díeȝle *av.* secretly (38)

díepe *f.sg.* the deep, sea (111)

díeran *I* love; praise, glorify: ȝe∼ endear (85)

díere *aj.av.* dear, precious, excellent, noble; dearly, expensively, kindly (85)

díerling (∼as) *m.* dear one, favorite (85)

diernan *I* conceal, keep secret (50)

dierne *n.sg.* secret: *aj.* secret, concealed (50)

ȝe-díersian *II* glorify (85)

dihtan *I* appoint, set (5)

á-dihtian *II* arrange (5)

á-dílegian *II* erase, blot out (6)

dimm *aj.* dark, dim (19)

á-dimmian *II* grow dim (19)

díofol (∼; díoflu) *m.n.* devil (75)

disc (∼as) *m.* dish, plate (2)

dogian *II* endure (?) (1)

dógor (∼) *m.n.* day (502)

dohte *see* dugan

dohtor (∼) *f.* daughter (44)

dol *aj.* foolish, arrogant, rash (19)

∼willen *n.sg.aj.* foolish(ness), rash(ness) (998)

dolfen *see* delfan

dolg (∼) *n.* wound (16)

dolgian *II* wound (16)

dóm (∼as) *m.* judgment, decree, opinion; justice, propriety; meaning, significance; authority, power; glory, glorious reputation (367)

-dóm *suff.* power, quality, condition (*of first element of compound*) (367)

dómian *II* glorify (367)

dón [<*dóan] (dyde/dǽde, ʒe-dón) *anv.* do, make, put (something) into or on-to (something); send: á~ remove, take out: be~ close: for~ destroy, ruin; ʒe~ do; make, consider: on~, un~ open (530)

dor (~u) *n.* portal, gate (37)

dorste *see* durran

draca (~n) *m.* dragon; the Devil (30)

dráf *see* drífan

dragan (ó, ó, a) *6* draw, go: be~ lead astray (3)

dranc *see* drincan

dréag *see* dréogan

dréam (~as) *m.* noisy merriment; music; gaiety, happiness (149)

dréas *see* dréosan

dreććan (dreahte) *I* oppress, annoy (13)

dréd *see* drǽdan

drenć *m.sg.* drink; drowning (76)

drenćan *I* cause to drink; drown (76)

drenće-flód (~a) *f.* deluge (122)

dreng (~as) *m.* young man, warrior (2)

dréogan (dréag, drugon, o) *2* experience, suffer; do, practice (91)

á-dréopan (éa, u, o) *2* fall in drops (9)

dréopian *II* drip (9)

dréor *m.sg.* gore, flowing blood (82)

~iʒ *aj.* dreary, wretched; cruel, horrid, grievous; bloody (?) (82)

dréoriʒian *II* be wretched, sad (82)

dréorung *f.sg.* falling, dropping (82)

dréosan (éa, druron, o) *2* fall, crumble, disintegrate: á~ decline: be~ deceive; deprive of: ʒe~ fall, decline (82)

ʒe-drep *n.sg.* blow, stroke (9)

drepan (æ, ǽ, e) *5* strike (9)

drepe *m.sg.* blow; slaying (9)

ʒe-drettan *I* consume (1)

dríeman *I* rejoice (149)

ʒe-dríeme *aj.* happy, joyful (149)

drífan (á, i, i) *1* drive, drive on, proceed; drive away, drive back; practice: á~ drive away, drive out: be~ drive, force; cover, surround: for~ drive out, drive on: in~ utter: to~ disperse, scatter; repel; destroy: þurh~ utter vehemently; pierce; permeate (62)

drinc/drynć (~as) *m.* drink (76)

drincan (a, u, u) *3* drink; be quenched (76)

drincend (~e) *m.* drinker (76)

dróf-líć *aj.* turbid, troubled (42)

dróg *see* dragan

drogen *see* dréogan

droht *m.n.sg.* way, condition of life (20)

~aþ, ~noþ *m.sg.* way, condition of life (20)

drohtian *II* lead one's life, conduct oneself (20)

dropa (~n) *m.* drop (9)

dropettan *I* drip, drop (9)

dropung (~a) *f.* dripping (9)

droren *see* dréosan

drúg (?) *m.sg.* dust (?) (18)

drúgian *II* become dry (18)

drugon *see* dréogan

druncen *n.sg.* drunkenness: *aj.* flushed by drink; drunken (76)

drunc-mennen *n.sg.* drunken maidservant (?), female drink-pourer (?) (1030)

druncon *see* drincan

druron *see* dréosan

drúsian *II* stagnate; sink, become low; droop (5)

drút *f.sg.* beloved one (1)

drý (~as) *m.* magician, wizard (8)

drýʒan *I* dry, dry up (18)

drýʒe *aj.* dry, arid (18)

dryht (~a) *f.* multitude, people, army, band of retainers; *pl.* men (1268)

~né (-néäs) *m.* warrior's corpse (4)

dryhten (dryhtnas) *m.* lord, ruler; the Lord (1268)

~bealu *n.sg.* great evil (94)

dryhtu (dryhta) *f.* nobility (1268)

drýman *I* be troubled (?) (1)

drynć *see* drinc

dryre *m.sg.* fall, lapse (82)

drysmian *II* grow dark, become gloomy (2)

on-drǽdan (é, é, ǽ) *7* dread, fear (39)

drǽfan *I* drive away, exile (62)

drǽfend (~) *m.* driver, hunter (62)

ʒe-drǽf-ness (~a) *f.* disturbance (62)

ʒe-drǽʒ *n.sg.* crowd; tumult (6)

drǽp *see* drepan

drœfan *I* excite, disturb (42)

ʒe-drœfed-ness (~a) *f.* tribulation (42)

dúfan (éa, u, o) *2* dive; sink; pierce (7)

dugan (déag, *def.* dohte) *prp.* be good, virtuous; be good for (something) (182)

duguþ (duguða) *f.* excellence; body of experienced retainers (*vs.* ʒeoguþ); people, men, multitude, army; majesty, power; prosperity, wealth; assistance, benefit, gift; decorum (182)

dulfon *see* delfan

dumb *aj.* speechless, dumb (15)

dún (~a, ~e) *f.* hill (25)

~scræf (-scrafu) *n.* mountain-cave (18)

dung (dynǵ) *f.* prison (1)

dunnian *II* become dark (?) (1)

durran (dearr, dearrst, dorste) *prp.* dare (37)

duru (dura) *f.* door (37)

dúst *n.sg.* dust (13)

dwelan (æ, ǽ, o) *4* go astray, err (3)

dwellan (dwealde) *I* prevent, hinder, mislead; go astray (33)

dweorg (~as) *m.* dwarf (1)

ʒe-dwield (~) *n.* error, heresy (33)

dwínan (á, i, i) *1* waste away (1)

dwol- *pref.* perverse, wrong (33)

ʒe-dwola (~n) *m.* error, heresy (33)

dwolen *see* dwelan

dwolma *m.sg.* chaos, confusion (33)

dwæl *see* dwelan

ʒe-dwǽs *aj.* stupid, foolish (1)

dwǽscan *I* extinguish (15)

dyde *see* dón

dyhtiʒ *aj.* doughty, strong (182)

dyn(e) *m.n.sg.* din, noise (18)

dynnan *I* make a din, noise (18)

dynt (~as) *m.* blow, stroke (2)

dyppan *I* dip, immerse (1)

ʒe-dyrst (~a) *f.* tribulation (?) (1)

dyrstiʒ *aj.* daring (37)

dysiʒ *n.sg.* folly, error: *aj.* foolish (24)

dysiʒian *II* act foolishly, err (24)

dys-líć, ~e *aj.av.* foolish(ly) (24)

dyttan *I* close, stop up (2)

dǽd (~e) *f.* deed, action (530)

~scua (~n) *m.* shadowy agent; the Devil (16)

dǽde *see* dón

dæʒ (dagas) *m.* day; time; name of D-rune (502)

~hwám *av.* daily (521)

~rǽd (~) *n.* daybreak (502)

~weorðung (~a) *f.* festival (227)

~willa *m.sg.* wished-for day (998)

~wóma *m.sg.* rush of day, dawn (40)

dæl (dalu) *n.* valley, dale (10)

dǽl (~as) *m.* part, share, a (great) deal (210)

~nimend *m.sg.* companion (180)

dǽlan *I* apportion, divide, separate; deprive; set free (210)

dærst(e) *f.sg.* leaven, ferment (1)

ʒe-dœfe *aj.av.* proper(ly), fitting(ly) (36)

dœma (~n) *m.* judge (367)

dœman *I* judge, adjudge, ordain; celebrate, praise; condemn (367)

Dœmend *m.sg.* Supreme Judge, God (367)

E

éa (~) *f.* water, flood, river, sea (44)

~let (?) *sg.* journey over the sea (?) (1)

éac *cj.* also, likewise, moreover: *prep.* in addition to (375) éaca (~n) *m.* addition, increase (375)

éacen *ppl.aj.* large, strong, vast; pregnant (375)

éacnian *II* grow large; become pregnant (375)

éacnung (~a) *f.* conception (375)

éad *n.sg.* wealth; good fortune; happiness; blessedness (241)

~(iȝ) *aj.* wealthy; fortunate; happy; blessed (241)

éaden *ppl.aj.* granted (241)

éaðe/íeðe (íeþ, éaðost) *av.* easily (141)

eafora (~n) *m.* heir, son (81)

eafoþ (eafoðu) *n.* power, strength (12)

éage (éagan) *n.* eye; sight (119)

éag-ȝe-byrd *f.sg.* nature of the eye (652)

éag-ȝe-mearc *n.sg.* horizon (73)

éagor- *pref.* water-, sea- (8)

eaht (~a) *f.* deliberation; esteem (30)

eahta *num.* eight (24)

eahtian *II* consider, esteem; guard, rule (30)

ȝe-eahtle (-eahtlan) *f.* esteem, regard (30)

eahtoða *aj.* eighth (24)

eahtung (~a) *f.* deliberation (30)

éa-lá *interj.* lo; alas (53)

eald (ieldra, ieldest) *aj.* old, ancient, ancestral (179)

~ȝe-seȝen (~a) *f.* old tradition, saga (380)

ealdian *II* grow old (179)

ealdor (ealdras) *m.* lord (298)

ealdor (~) *n.* life; eternity (298)

~legu *f.sg.* death, destiny (160)

eald(or)-wǽriȝ *aj.* very (?), fatally (?), weary (103)

ealgian *II* defend (7)

ealh (~as) *m.* (heathen) temple (2)

eall *sb.aj.av.* everything; all; altogether, utterly (1600)

~es *av.* entirely (1600)

~ing *av.* always, regularly (1600)

~inga, -unga *av.* altogether, entirely (1600)

ealneȝ *av.* always (1600)

ealu *n.sg.* ale, beer (8)

~scierwen *f.sg.* terror, despair; serving of (bitter, fateful) drink (?); deprivation of ale, of prosperity, of revelry (?) (52)

~wosa *m.sg.* ale-drinker (4189)

éam (~as) *m.* maternal uncle (2)

éar (~as) *m.* sea, water (9)

éar *m.sg.* earth, grave; name of EA-rune (1)

earc, ~e *m.f.sg.* chest; ark (17)

eard (~as) *m.* land, dwelling, estate, home; condition, fate (200)

~lufu (-lufan) *f.* beloved home (426)

eardian *II* dwell; inhabit; remain (200)

eardung (~a) *f.* habitation (200)

éare (éaran) *n.* ear (for hearing) (22)

éarendel *m.sg.* rising sun (1)

earfeðe *aj.* difficult (78)

earfoþ(e) (earfoðu) *n.* hardship, difficulty (78)

~háwe *aj.* seen with difficulty, imperceptible (1)

~tǽcne *aj.* difficult to be shown, undemonstrable (77)

earg *aj.* cowardly, weak; useless, slothful, vile (10)

earh *f.sg.* arrow (7)

~faru (-fara) *f.* flight of arrows; attack (366)

earm (~as) *m.* arm (of the body) (18)

earm, ~e *aj.av.* poor(ly), wretched(ly) (169)

~scæpen *aj.* wretched (340)

earn (~as) *m.* eagle (20)

earn *see* iornan

earnian *II* earn, merit (30)

earnung (~a) *f.* desert, merit (30)

earu *aj.* quick, active (2)

earwunga *av.* gratuitously (4)

éast *aj.av.* east, easterly, eastward (47)

éastan *av.* from the east (47)

Éaster- *pref.* Easter (47)

éasterne *aj.* eastern, oriental (47)

éawan/íewan *I* show, present, reveal (82)

éawunga *av.* face to face (82)

eax *f.sg.* axle (4)

eaxl (~a) *f.* shoulder (27)

~ʒe-spann *n.sg.* intersection of the beams of a cross (6)

~ʒe-stealla (~n) *m.* shoulder-companion, comrade (16)

éaþ- *pref.* easily (141)

~be-ʒíete *aj.* easily had; prepared, ready (166)

~bǽde *aj.* easy to entreat; exorable (150)

~fynde *aj.* easily (to be) found, seen, heard; ("many a . . ." [?]; "prominent, conspicuous, very audible" [?]) (148)

~ʒe-síene *aj.* easily seen; conspicuous (?); plentiful (?) (494)

~mód, -mǿde *aj.* gentle, gracious, humble (840)

~mǿdu *n.pl.* humility (840)

~mǿttu (-mǿtta) *f.* humility (840)

ʒe-éaþ-mǿdan *I* humble oneself (840)

ebba (~n) *m.* ebb-tide (4)

ebbian *II* ebb, flow out (4)

éće *see* óće

ećed (~) *n.* vinegar (2)

ecg (~a) *f.* edge, (sword-)edge (92)

ed- *pref.* again, anew, back (77)

~hwyrft (~as) *m.* turning, reversal (of fortune) (207)

~scæft *f.sg.* regeneration (340)

~wend(en) *f.sg.* reversal, change (213)

~wielm *m.sg.* whirlpool (130)

~wihte *f.(?)sg.* anything, any way (?) (245)

~wít (~) *n.* blame, reproach (225)

~wít-stæf (-stafas) *m.* reproach, disgrace (40)

ʒe-ed-byrdan *I* generate (652)

edisc (~as) *m.* enclosed pasture (11)

edring (?) *f.sg.* refuge (?) (11)

efen *aj.* parallel, level, even with (110)

~(e) *av.* just, even (110)

~pynde (?) *aj.* continually or greatly pent up, dammed (?) (2)

efenettan *I* make equal (110)

efnan *I* accomplish, cause; make, prepare; suffer, sustain (37)

eft *av.* in turn, again, later (316)

eʒe *m.sg.* fear, terror (218)

eʒesa (~n) *m.* terror (218)

eʒesan *av.* very, terribly (218)

eʒesian *II* terrify (218)

eʒesiʒ *aj.* terrifying, terrible (218)

egl *f.sg.* spike; talon, claw (1)

eʒlan *I* grieve, molest (13)

eʒle *aj.* hateful, hideous (13)

elcor(a) *av.* otherwise (74)

el(l)- *pref.* from elsewhere, alien (74)

~lende *aj.* foreign, wandering (231)

~reordiʒ *aj.* of foreign speech, barbarous (79)

~þéodiʒ *aj.* of an alien people, foreign (460)

ellen *m.n.sg.* valor, strength (122)

ellen- *intensive pref.* very, powerful, great (122)

~wód *f.sg.* zeal: *aj.* raging, furious (8)

elles *av.* otherwise, else (74)

~hwerʒen *av.* elsewhere (136)

ellne *av.dat.* quickly (122)

ellnian *II* emulate; comfort (122)

ellor *av.* elsewhere (74)

ellra *comp.aj.* another (74)

eln (~a) *f.* ell (measure), forearm (2)

end *av.* formerly (154)

-end(e) *suff. (forms agent nouns from vbs.)*

ende (endas) *m.* end; sea-coast (154)

~byrd *f.sg.* order, plan (652)

~byrdnes *av.* properly (652)

~stæf (-stafas) *m.* end (40)

~sǽta *m.sg.* coast-guard (495)

ʒe-ende-byrdan *I* order, dispose (652)

endemes *av.* equally, uniformly (2)

endian *II* come to an end; bring to an end; bring about (154)

~end-leofan *num.* eleven (1)

enʒe *aj.av.* narrow, confined, anxious, troubled; anxiously (16)

enʒel (enʒlas) *m.* angel (305)

Engle *m.pl.* the English (11)

Englisc *aj.* English (11)

enġu (enġe) *f.* narrowness, confinement (16)

ent (~as) *m.* giant (9)

entisc *aj.* gigantic, made by giants (9)

éode *see* gán

eodor (~as) *m.* enclosure, precinct, dwelling; vault, sky; protection, protector, prince (11)

~gang *m.sg.* a quest for home, protection (264)

eofol-sǽċ *n.sg.* blasphemy (1)

eofor (~as) *m.* boar, boar-image (11)

eofot *n.sg.* sin (1)

eoh (~) *m.n.* steed; name of short E-rune (11)

eolh-secg *m.sg.* reed, sedge; papyrus (?); sea-holly (?); name of Z-rune (1)

eorc(n)an-, eorclan-stán (~as) *m.* precious stone (5)

eorðe (eorðan) *f.* earth (as material), the Earth (625)

eorl (~as) *m.* noble warrior; (Norse) jarl, earl (of England) (216)

eormen/iermen *aj.* great, powerful, spacious (8)

eornost *f.sg.* earnestness, zeal (7)

eornoste *aj.av.* earnest(ly), serious(ly) (7)

éorod *n.sg.* troop of horsemen (11)

eorp *aj.* dark (9)

eorþ- *pref.* of the earth (625)

~búend(e) *m.pl.* dwellers on the earth; men; natives of a country (*sc.* Frisia) (114)

eosol (~as) *m.* ass, donkey (1)

eoten (~as) *m.* giant (8)

eotenisc *aj.* gigantic, made by giants (8)

éowde *f.sg.* flock of sheep (6)

erian *I* till (the soil) (1)

erinaces *m.pl.* (*Lat.*) hedgehogs (1)

eruca *f.sg.*(?) (for *Lat.* eruca) colewort, cabbage (?); caterpillar (?) (1)

esne (esnas) *m.* servant, man (40)

etan (ǽ, ǽ, e) *5*(*irreg.*) eat; corrode (65)

F

fácen (~) *n.* deceit (92)

~ȝe-swipere *m.sg.* scourge of false counsel (8)

~stæf (-stafas) *m.* treachery (40)

fág *aj.* colored, stained; blood-stained; shining; variegated (42)

fágian *II* vary, change, shine (42)

fáh *aj.* hostile; guilty, criminal, outlawed (108)

fám *n.sg.* foam (29)

~iȝ *aj.* foamy (29)

fámiȝan *II* foam (29)

fana (~n) *m.* flag, banner, standard (2)

fand *see* findan

fandian *II* try, attempt; search out; experience (9)

fandung (~a) *f.* trial, investigation (9)

fangen *see* fón

fara (~n) *m.* traveler (366)

ȝe-fara (~n) *m.* (traveling) companion (366)

faran (ó, ó, a) *6* go, journey, die: á~ go out, depart, travel: be~ surround: ȝe~ go, travel, attain; act, behave; die: ȝeond~ pervade; traverse: ofer~ pass over, traverse: oþ~ escape: to~ separate, scatter: wiþ~ escape (366)

faroþ (faroðas) *m.* water in motion, sea; surf; beach, shore (366)

faru (fara) *f.* passage, journey, march; expedition; movable possessions (366)

féa *aj.av.* few, a few; little (31)

~lóg *aj.* destitute (1)

~scæft *aj.* destitute, helpless, poor (340)

ȝe-féa (~n) *m.* joy (102)

feaȝ *see* féon

feaht *see* feohtan

-feald *suff.* -fold (27)

ȝe-feald (?) *n.sg.* region, dwelling-place (?) (27)

fealdan (éo, éo, ea) *7* fold (27)

fealh *see* féolan

feall *n.sg.* fall, death (141)

feallan (éo, éo, ea) *7* fall; befall; fall down, fail: be~ fall; deprive (141)

fealu *aj.* dark (23)

fealwian *II* grow dark (23)

fearh *m.sg.* boar (?) (1)

fearm (~as) *m.* freight, cargo (1)

fearn (~) *n.* fern (1)

feax *n.sg.* hair: *suff.* -haired (19)

feććan (feah) *I* fetch, seize (79)

feðer (~a) *f.* feather (56)

ʒe-feðrian *II* provide with feathers, wings (56)

fefer *m.n.sg.* fever (1)

feʒen *see* féon

fela *indecl.n.* much (of), large amount (of); *aj.av.* great(ly) (246)

fela- *intensive pref.* very, much (246)

feld (~as) *m.* open country, field, pasture (26)

fell (~) *n.* skin, hide (5)

fell *aj.* cruel, fierce (1)

fenġ (~as) *m.* grip, grasp (198)

féng *see* fón

fenġel (fenġlas) *m.* lord, prince (3)

fenix *m.sg.* phoenix (3)

fenn (~as) *m.* marsh, fen (8)

feoh (~) *n.* cattle, property, wealth; name of F-rune (47)

feoht (~) *n.* fight, battle (65)

feohtan (ea, u, o) *3* fight, gain by fighting, win; grapple with, grope (65)

feohte (feohta) *f.* fight, battle (65)

féolan [<*feolhan] (fealh, fǽlon, o) *3* enter, penetrate, press on: be~ put away, bury; deliver, commit to: ʒeond~ fill: æt~ adhere, cling to; keep close to (20)

féold *see* fealdan

féoll *see* feallan

ʒe-féon [<*feohan <*fehan] (feaʒ, fǽgon, feʒen) *5* rejoice (102)

feorh (fĕoras; feorh) *m.n.* life, spirit; life-blood (325)

~góma (?) (~n) *m.* fatal jaws (?) (13)

~góme (?) (-góman) *f.* subsistence (?) (13)

~legu *f.sg.* death, destiny (160)

~rǽd *m.sg.* salvation (174)

feorm (~a) *f.* feeding, sustenance, entertainment; possessions (30)

feormian *II* feed, entertain; consume; clean, scour (30)

feormiend (~) *m.* host, entertainer; cleaner, polisher (30)

feormung (~a) *f.* provision (30)

feorr (*av.comp.* fierr) *aj.av.* far; far back in time (80)

feorran *av.* from afar, from long ago (80)

feorsian *II* depart (80)

féower *num.* four (80)

~tíene *num.* fourteen (24)

~tiʒ *num.* forty (24)

féo(we)rða *aj.* fourth (80)

féowung *f.sg.* rejoicing (102)

ferhþ (~as; ~) *m.n.* mind, life, spirit (183)

ferian *I* carry; lead; go, depart (366)

feriend *m.sg.* leader (366)

fers (~) *n.* verse (2)

fersian *II* versify (2)

fetel (~as) *m.* belt (2)

~hilt *f.sg.* sword with ring-hilt (2)

ʒe-feterian *II* fetter (79)

fetian *II* fetch, seize (79)

fetor (~a) *f.* fetter, bond (79)

ʒe-fic (~) *n.* deceit (92)

fíc-béam (~as) fig-tree (1)

fiðer- *pref.* four (80)

fiðere (fiðeru) *n.* wing (56)

ʒe-fiðrian *II* provide with feathers, wings (56)

fiell (~as) *m.* fall, death (141)

fiellan *I* fell, lay low, kill (141)

fierd (~a) *f.* armed force, militia, levy (50)

fierʒen- *pref.* mountain, mountain-woodland (9)

fierr *see* feorr

á-fierran *I* remove (to afar) (80)

fiersian *II* remove to a distance; do without (80)

fiersn (~a) *f.* heel (1)

fíf *num.* five (46)

~mæȝen (~) *n.* quintuple (magic) power (1596)

~ta *aj.* fifth (46)

~tíene *num.* fifteen (24)

~tiȝ *num.* fifty (24)

fífel (~) *n.* (sea-)monster (4)

fille *f.sg.* chervil, *Anthriscus cerefolium* (1)

findan (fand/funde, u, u) *3* find, discover, meet; arrange, devise, invent; experience, find out; seek out; visit: ~(æt) obtain from, prevail upon: á~ experience, sense: on~ find out, perceive; experience; get, obtain (148)

finger (fingras) *m.* finger (14)

finol *m.sg.* fennel, *Foeniculum vulgare* (1)

finta (~n) *m.* tail; consequence (3)

fío(ga)n *I* hate, persecute (320)

fíol (~a) *f.* file, rasp (3)

fíond (~as; fíend) *m.* enemy; the fiend (Satan) (320)

fíowung *f.sg.* hatred, enmity (320)

fíras *m.pl.* men, mankind (325)

firen (~a) *f.* crime, sin; suffering, torment (180)

~líć, ~e *aj.av.* wicked; rashly, vehemently (322)

firenian *II* sin; rebuke (180)

firenum *av.dat.* wickedly; very, exceedingly (180)

first *av.* at first (29)

first *see* frist

fisc (~as) *m.* fish (26)

fitt (~a) *f.* song, poem (4)

fitt *n.sg.* fight, contest (4)

flá (~n) *f.* arrow (21)

flacor *aj.* flying (2)

fláh *n.sg.* evil, treachery: *aj.* deceitful, hostile (5)

flán (~a) *f.* arrow (21)

flát *see* flítan

fléag *see* fléogan

fléah *see* fléon

fléam (~as) *m.* flight (to safety) (31)

fléan [<*fleahan <*flahan] (flóg, ó, a) *6* flay (1)

fléat *see* fléotan

fleax *n.sg.* flax (1)

fléogan (fléag, flugon, o) *2* fly; flee (123)

fléoge (fléogan) *f.* fly, insect (123)

fléoh *n.sg.* fly, insect (123)

fléon (fléah, flugon, o) *2* flee, escape, avoid; put to flight: ofer~ flee from (123)

fléot (~as) *m.* raft, vessel (34)

fléotan (éa, u, o) *2* float, swim, sail (34)

fléow *see* flówan

flett (~) *n.* floor (of hall or common-room) (25)

~ȝe-steald (~) *n.* household goods (14)

flíema (~n) *m.* refugee, fugitive, exile, outlaw (31)

flíeman *I* put to flight, rout (31)

flíes (~) *n.* fleece (3)

flint (~as) *m.* flint (5)

ȝe-flit (~u) *n.* contest, altercation (14)

flita (~n) (?) *m.* contestant (?) (14)

flítan (á, i, i) *1* contend, compete: ofer~ overcome in contest (14)

flócan (éo, éo, ó) *7* clap, applaud (1)

flód (~as) *m.* tide, sea, flood (122)

-floga (~n) *m.suff.* flier (123)

flogen *see* fléogan, fléon

flór (~as) *m.* floor, pavement; bottom (of a body of water) (10)

flot *n.sg.* deep water, sea (34)

flota (~n) *m.* ship; sailor (34)

ȝe-flota (~n) *m.* whale (34)

floten *see* fléotan

flówan (éo, éo, ó) *7* flow (25)

flugon *see* fléogan, fléon

fluton *see* fléotan

flyȝe *m.sg.* flight (123)

flyht (~as) *m.* flight, flying (123)

flǽsc *n.sg.* flesh, the fleshly body (67)

flœ́de *aj.* in flood, overflowing (122)

fnæd (fnadu) *n.* fringe, border (1)

fnǽst *m.sg.* blast, breath (2)

fódor *n.sg.* food, fodder (62)

ȝe-fóg (~) *n.* joint, fitting (21)

fohten *see* feohtan

folc (~) *n.* people, tribe, nation; armed force (430)

~rǽd *m.sg.* benefit of the people (174)

folde (foldan) *f.* earth; surface of the Earth; soil; land, region (224)

folen *see* féolan

folgere (folgeras) *m.* follower, retainer (41)

folgian *II* follow, persue; serve, obey (41)

folgoþ/folgaþ (folgoðas) *m.* following, retinue; way of life (41)

folm (~a) *f.* palm of the hand, hand (62)

fón [<*fóhan<*fanhan] (féng, é, a) ⁊ grasp, seize, take; undertake: be~ grasp, comprehend, encompass, envelop: ymb~ grasp, surround: þurh~ get through, penetrate (198)

for *prep.* for, on account of; before, in the presence of, in the sight of; in return for; in place of (807)

~hwon *cj.* because (531)

~hwý *instr.pron.* wherefore (521)

~weard *m.sg. (?)* agreement, covenant (?): *av.(?)* in future, continually (?) (140; 882)

for- *pref.* (*intensive; pejorative*) (223)

~dón *ppl.aj.* corrupt, wicked (530)

~ȝief-ness (~a) *f.* gift; forgiveness (396)

~hogod-ness (~a) *f.* contempt (571)

~hæfed-ness *f.* self-restraint, abstinence (771)

~lor *n.sg.* loss (224)

~maniȝ *aj.* very many (275)

~scæp *n.sg.* evil deed (340)

~woren *ppl.aj.* decayed, decrepit (1)

~wyrht (~u) *n.* sin (538)

~þylman *I* wrap up, enclose (3)

fór *f.sg.* going, journey; way of life (366)

fór *see* faran

foran *av.prep.* before, ahead, forward; before, opposite (223)

ford *m.sg.* ford; sea (3)

ȝe-forðian *II* carry out, perform (237)

fore *av.* before, beforehand, formerly: *prep.* for, before, in the presence of, on account of (223)

fore- *pref.* fore-, before; very (223)

~rynel (~as) *m.* fore-runner, morning star (41)

for(e)weard *aj.av.* forward, in front, fore, early; toward the future (882)

forht *aj.* frightened, afraid; frightful, terrible (89)

forhtian *II* become frightened; frighten (89)

forma *aj.* first (223)

forod *ppl.aj.* broken, violated (2)

forst (~as) *m.* frost (20)

forþ *av.* forth, forward, on(ward); away; henceforth (237)

forþ- *pref.* "forth-," forward, preeminent (237)

~bǽru *f.sg.* productivity (652)

~ȝe-scæft (~a) *f.* creation, destiny, the future (340)

~spell (~) *n.* declaration, pronouncement (66)

~weard *m.sg.* pilot (257)

~weard *aj.* inclined forward; enduring (882)

fóstor *m.sg.* food, sustenance (2)

fót (fǽt) *m.* foot (79)

fox *m.sg.* fox (1)

fracŭþ (fracŭðu) *n.* insult, scorn (539)

fracŭþ, fracŭðe *aj.av.* wicked, hateful; shamefully (539)

fram *aj.* active, bold, brave (282)

fram *av.* from, away, forth: *prep.* from, away from; as a result of; about, concerning (245)

franca (~n) *m.* (Frankish spear) (4)

frásian *II* ask, require (2)

frásung (~a) f. asking, tempting (2)
fréa (~n) m. lord; the Lord (203)
fréa- *intensive pref.* very, exceedingly (203)
frec aj. greedy; bold (18)
freca (~n) m. bold one, warrior (18)
freću f.sg. craving (18)
freʒen see fricgan
freʒn n.sg. question (155)
freme aj. good, excellent, kind (282)
frem(e)ðe aj. alien, foreign, strange, estranged from (41)
fremman I accomplish, do, further, express (a feeling or attitude) (282)
-fremmend(e) ppl.suff. -doer, -maker (282)
fremsum, ~e aj.av. kind(ly), gracious(ly) (282)
fremu (frema) f. goodness, excellence, kindness (282)
fréoriʒ aj. freezing cold; sad, mournful (16)
fréosan (fréas, fruron, o) 2 freeze (16)
fretan (ǽ, ǽ, e) 5(irreg.) devour, eat; break (65)
frićća (~n) m. herald (155)
fricgan (fræʒ, frǽgon, freʒen) 1-5 ask; ascertain (155)
friclan I desire (8)
fríd-henʒest (~as) m. stately horse (64)
friða (~n) m. protector (105)
friðian II make peace; protect, cherish (105)
friðu f.sg. peace, security (105)
fríʒe f.pl. love, passion (141)
friʒnan (æ, frugnon, u) 3 inquire; learn (by asking) (155)
frío f.sg. lady (64)
frío aj. free, noble, generous; joyful (64)
fríod (~a) f. love, peace (141)
frío(ʒa)n (fríode) I set free; honor; like, love (141)
fríon see fríoʒan
fríond (~as; fríend) m. friend (141)
frist/first f.sg. space of time, appointed time (29)
friþ m.n.sg. peace, security (105)
fród aj. wise, experienced; old (80)
fródian II be wise (80)
frófor (frófra) f. consolation, help (118)
frówe (frówan) f. lady (203)
frugnon see friʒnan
frum- pref. first-, original (224)
~cynn (~) n. descent, lineage; tribe, race (389)
~gár, -gára (~as; ~n) m. chieftain, leader (100)
~scæft (~a) f. creation; origin, original state; creature (340)
fruma (~n) m. beginning; inventor, creator, cause; chief, leader (224)
frumþ/frymþ (~as) m. origin, creation, first fruits (224)
frymdiʒ aj. desirous, inquiring (1)
frymþ see frumþ
ʒe-frǽʒe n.sg. information, knowledge: aj. renowned (155)
frǽʒn see friʒnan
frǽte, frǽtiʒ aj. perverse, proud (3)
frætwa (~n) m. adorner (88)
frætwa f.pl. treasures, trappings (88)
frætw(i)an I-II adorn (88)
frœ́ćen (~) n. danger (75)
frœ́cne aj.av. bold(ly), dangerous(ly), wicked(ly), savage(ly) (75)
ʒe-frœ́cnian II make bold (75)
frœ́fr(i)an I-II console (118)
fugol (fuglas) m. bird (96)
~timber n.sg. young bird (96)
fuhton see feohtan
fúl (~) n. foulness, guilt: aj. foul, impure (18)
full n.sg. beaker, cup (12)
full aj.av. full(y) (232)
full- pref. full, complete (232)
~lǽst (~as) m. aid (72)
~wíht m.sg. baptism (18)
-full aj.suff. full, full of (232)
fullian II fulfill, complete (232)
fultum m.sg. help (79)

fultumian *II* help; be gracious to (79)

fulwian *II* baptize (18)

funde, fundon *see* findan

fundian *II* try, attempt (21)

furðor *av.* further (237)

furðum *av.* at first, just (of time); even, indeed, exactly, just as (23)

fús *aj.* striving forward, eager; shining; brave; ready for death; mortal (93)

~léoþ (~) *n.* death-song (28)

fylće *n.sg.* people, land (430)

fylȝan (fylȝde) *I* follow, pursue, persecute; persist in; attend to, observe (41)

fyllan *I* fill, fulfill (232)

fyllaþ *m.sg.* fill, plenty (232)

fyllend (~) *m.* one who fulfills (232)

fyllu *f.sg.* plenty, fill (of food); impregnation (232)

fylst *m.f.sg.* help, aid (7)

fylstan *I* aid, help (7)

fýlþ *f.sg.* filth, impurity (18)

fýr (~) *n.* fire (190)

fyrðran *I* advance, further (237)

fýren *aj.* fiery, burning (190)

fyrht *aj.* frightened (89)

á-fyrhtan *I* affright, terrify (89)

fyrhtu (fyrhta) *f.* fright (89)

fyrmest *aj.av.* first, foremost; first, at first, most, especially (223)

fyrn *aj.av.* former, ancient; long ago, formerly (80)

fyrs (~as) *m.* furze (1)

fyr-witt *n.sg.* curiosity (10)

fýsan *I* impel, hasten (93)

fýst (~a) *f.* fist (3)

fæc (facu) *n.* interval or space of time (10)

fǽcne *aj.* deceitful; old (?): *av.* maliciously; disgracefully; exceedingly (92)

fæder (~) *m.* father (252)

fædera (~n) *m.* paternal uncle (252)

fæderen- *pref.* paternal, from the father's side (252)

fæðm (~as) *m.* embrace, protection, bosom (63)

fæðm(i)an *I–II* embrace, surround (63)

ȝe-fæȝ *aj.* pleasing, dear (14)

fǽȝe *aj.* fated to die, doomed (51)

fæȝen *aj.* glad, willing (14)

fǽȝer *aj.av.* fair(ly), pleasant(ly), beautiful(ly) (198)

fæȝnian *II* be glad, rejoice (14)

fæȝrian *II* grow fair, become beautiful (198)

fǽhþ(u) (fǽhþa) *f.* hostility, revenge, feud (108)

fæl *see* féolan

fǽle *aj.av.* faithful(ly), good; well (43)

-fǽle *aj.suff.* frightful, terrible (3)

fǽlon *see* féolan

fǽlsian *II* cleanse, purify; pass through, traverse (9)

á-fǽman *I* breathe out (29)

fǽmne (fǽmnan) *f.* maiden, virgin, bride (46)

fær (faru) *n.* vehicle, vessel; expedition; way (366)

fǽr *m.sg.* sudden attack; danger (66)

fǽr- *pref.* sudden, intense (66)

á-fǽran *I* frighten (66)

fǽreld *n.sg.* journey (366)

fǽringa *av.* suddenly (66)

fæsl *n.sg.(?)* progeny (3)

fæst, ~e *aj.av.* firm(ly), fast (372)

~gangol *aj.* faithful, constant (264)

~hafol-ness *f.sg.* stinginess (771)

~rǽd *aj.* firmly resolved (174)

~steall *aj.* standing firmly (16)

-fæst *aj.suff.* firm in, fixed in (372)

fæstan *I* fasten; establish; commit, entrust: be~ fasten; establish; commend: oþ~ entrust, commit to another; inflict: æt~ fasten, fix; afflict (372)

fæstan *I* fast; expiate by fasting; abstain from (7)

fæsten (~) *n.* fastness, safe retreat, stronghold, prison (372)

fæsten (~) *n.* fast; abstinence (7)

fæstnian *II* fasten, secure (372)

fæstnung (~a) *f.* strengthening, security (372)

fæt *m.sg.* path, way; experience (17)

fæt (fatu) *n.* container, vessel, vat (31)

fǽt (~) *n.* plate-metal, gold ornament (15)

fǽted *aj.* ornamented with gold (15)

fǽtels *m.sg.* bag, receptacle (31)

fætt *aj.* fat (5)

fœ́dan *I* nurture, feed; bring forth (62)

fœ́ða (~n) *m.* foot-soldier, troop (39)

fœ́ðe *n.sg.* walking, gait, pace (39)

fœ́ȝan *I* join, fit together (21)

fœ́lan *I* feel, touch (3)

ȝe-fœ́ra (~n) *m.* companion, comrade (366)

fœ́ran *I* journey, go: ȝe~ journey, go; reach, obtain; experience, suffer; behave, act (366)

ȝe-fœ́re *aj.* accessible (366)

fœ́rend (~) *m.* messenger, sailor (366)

fœ́ring (~a) *f.* journey (366)

fœ́r-ness (~a) *f.* crossing, passage (366)

ȝe-fœ́r-sciepe (-sciepas) *m.* fellowship, society (340)

G–3

gád *f.sg.* goad, point (1)

gád/gǽd *n.sg.* lack (6)

gader *see* ȝeador

gadrian *II* collect, gather, assemble (86)

gafol *n.sg.* tax, tribute, due (12)

gál *n.sg.* wantonness, lechery; evil: *aj.* wanton; happy (38)

~sciepe *m.sg.* folly (340)

galan (ó, ó, a) *6* sing; cry out; enchant (43)

gambe (gamban) *f.* tribute, tax (2)

gamelian *II* grow old (27)

gamen *n.sg.* mirth, sport (14)

gamol *aj.* old (27)

gán [<* gáan] (éode, ȝe-gán) *anv.* go, come, walk; come about: á~ come to pass, appear: be~ cultivate, practise:

full~ accomplish, fulfill; follow, assist: ȝe~ go, go to; gain, win; bring to pass; happen: of~ avoid: ofer~ traverse, overrun: oþ~ go away, escape: ymb~ go around (135)

gán *see* ȝínan

gang (~as) *m.* pace, gait; course, way; attack (264)

gangan (ȝéong, éo, gangen) *7* go, walk; come about, happen: be~ perform, practise; worship: ȝe~ go, happen, befall; accomplish, obtain (264)

-gangende *ppl.suff.* -going, -walking (264)

gange-wifre *f.sg.* "traveling weaver," spider (16)

-gann *see* -ȝinnan

ganot (~as) *m.* gannet, the solan goose (4)

gár (~as) *m.* spear, arrow, javelin; agony (?); storm (?); name of velar G-rune (100)

~secg *m.sg.* sea, stormy (?) sea (22)

gás-ríć *m.sg.* raging, impetuous being (?) (1)

gást *see* gǽst

gást-bana (~n) *m.* soul-slayer, the Devil (111)

ȝé *pron.* ye, you (15974)

ȝĕ, ȝĕ . . . ȝĕ *cj.* and, also; both . . . and, either . . . or (19)

ȝe- *pref.* (*often without meaning: or signifies association; completion of action; perfective result*)

ȝéac (~as) *m.* cuckoo (3)

ȝeador/gader *av.* together (86)

~tang *aj.* continuous, united (25)

ȝeaf *see* ȝiefan

ȝéagl (~as) *m.* jaws (1)

ȝeald *see* ȝieldan

ȝealdor (ȝealdru) *n.* enchantment, spell, incantation, song (43)

ȝealga (~n) *m.* gallows; cross of Christ (16)

ȝealg-mód *aj.* mournful (1)

ȝealg-tréo (-tréowu) *n.* gallows-tree (16)

ʒeall *see* ʒiellan
ʒealp *see* ʒielpan
ʒealla (~n) *m.* gall (2)
ʒéanoþ *m.f.n.* complaint, lament (1)
ʒéap *aj.* curved; spacious; broad (14)
ʒéap *see* ʒéopan
ʒéar (~) *n.* year, beginning or spring of the year; summer, harvest; name of early [j]- or yod-rune (84)
~dagas *m.pl.* former days, time past (502)
ʒéara *av.* of yore, formerly (84)
ʒeard (~as) *m.* enclosure; court-yard; dwelling (167)
ʒeare *see* ʒearwe, *av.*
ʒearu *aj.* ready, prepared, complete (225)
~folm *aj.* with ready hand (62)
ʒéarum *av.* formerly (84)
ʒearwe *f.pl.* gear, clothing, arms (225)
ʒearwe/ʒeare *av.* readily; indeed; entirely; well (225)
ʒearwian *II* make ready, prepare (225)
ʒeat (~u) *n.* gate (15)
-ʒeat, ʒéat *see* -ʒietan, ʒéotan
ʒeato-líć *aj.* equipped, adorned; noble (26)
ʒeatwan *I* equip, adorn (26)
ʒeatwe *f.pl.* equipment, trappings (26)
ʒéaþ (ʒéaða) *f.* foolishness; scorn (4)
ʒeʒn *av.* still, again (29)
ʒeʒnum *av.* forward; directly (29)
ʒeʒnunga *av.* directly, wholly, altogether, immediately (29)
ʒén(a) *see* ʒeona
-genʒa (~n) *m.* mover, walker (264)
genʒan *I* go, ride (264)
genʒe *aj.* going, current, effectual, valid; usual, agreeable, convenient (264)
ʒéo/íu *av.* of yore, long ago, formerly (38)
~méowle *f.sg.* woman of old (11)
~scæft *f.sg.* what was decreed of old, destiny (340)
~scæft-gást (~as) *m.* doomed spirit (408)
ʒeoc (~u) *n.* yoke (2)

ʒéoc (~a) *f.* help, safety, consolation (37)
ʒéocend *m.sg.* helper, the Saviour (37)
ʒéocian *II* help, save, preserve (37)
ʒéocor *aj.* severe, harsh; bitter, sad (7)
ʒéocre *av.* harshly (7)
ʒeofian *II* endow (396)
ʒeofon *n.sg.* sea, ocean (31)
ʒeoguþ (ʒeoguða) *f.* youth, young (vs. veteran) retainers; *cp.* duguþ (51)
ʒeohhol *n.sg.* Yule; December and January (1)
ʒeoloca (~n) *m.* yolk, yellow of an egg (4)
ʒeolu *aj.* yellow (4)
ʒéomor, ~e *aj.av.* sad(ly), mournful(ly), wretched(ly) (72)
ʒéomrian *II* lament, be sad (72)
ʒeona/ʒén(a) *av.* yet, still, further (70)
ʒeond *prep.* through, throughout, over, among, along, beyond (194)
ʒeond- *vb.pref.* throughout, widely (194)
ʒeong (ʒienʒra, ʒienʒest) *aj.* young (188)
ʒéong *see* gangan
ʒeongor-dóm, -sciepe *m.sg.* discipleship (367; 340)
ʒéopan (éa, gupon, o) *2* take in, swallow (1)
ʒeorn, ~e *aj.av.* eager, desirous; eagerly, zealously, carefully, exactly, well (228)
ʒeostran *aj.av.* yesterday (4)
ʒéotan (éa, guton, o) *2* pour, pour out, flow, rush (as water); found, cast: á~ pour out, shed, flow; drain, deprive of; consume, destroy: be~ pour over, cover with: ʒe~ found, cast: þurh~ endue (42)
ʒeoxa (~n) *m.* sob (1)
ʒér-sciepe *m.sg.* joke, merriment (?) (1)
ʒicel (~as) *m.* icicle (4)
ʒiedd (~) *n.* poem, lay, traditional short poem; utterance (40)
ʒieddian *II* recite a lay; speak; sing (40)
ʒieddung (~a) *f.* song, poem, saying (40)
ʒief *cj.* if; though; whether (327)
ʒief- *pref.* gift-, of a gift (396)

~fæst *aj.* gifted (372)

~heall *f.sg.* hall in which generosity is practised (41)

~ness (~a) *f.* benefit, favor, grace (396)

~scætt (~as) *m.* valuable gift (12)

~stól (~as) *m.* throne (51)

ȝiefa (~n) *m.* giver (396)

ȝiefan (ea, éa, ie) *5* give: á~ give, give back, give up, leave: for~ give, grant; forgive; give up, cease: of~ give up, abandon: æt~ offer, provide (396)

ȝiefeðe *n.sg.* lot, fate: *aj.* granted (396)

ȝiefian *II* endow (396)

ȝiefl (~) *n.* morsel (9)

ȝiefu (ȝiefa) *f.* gift, giving, favor; generosity, grace; name of palatal G-rune (396)

ȝiehþ(u) (ȝiehþa) *f.* grief (15)

ȝield (~) *n.* payment, compensation; substitute; sacrifice, worship; god, idol (122)

ȝieldan (ea, guldon, o) *3* pay, repay; worship, sacrifice to: á~ pay, grant, be granted; repay, punish: for~ requite, reward; release, give up: ȝe~ repay: on~ pay, be punished for; pay offer (122)

-ȝiell *aj.suff.* broad, extensive (6)

ȝiellan (ea, gullon, o) *3* scream, yell; sing out (43)

ȝielp *m.n.sg.* glory, pride, boast (58)

ȝielpan (ea, gulpon, o) *3* boast; rejoice (58)

ȝielpen *aj.* boastful (58)

ȝieman *I* care about, attend to (32)

ȝieme-léas *aj.* heedless (224)

ȝiemen (~a) *f.* care, heed (32)

ȝiemend (~) *m.* ruler (32)

ȝien(a) *av.* yet, still, further (70)

ȝienȝra (~n) *m.* youth; follower, servant disciple: *f.sg.* handmaid (188)

ȝiepe *aj.* clever (1)

ȝierd *f.sg.* rod, staff (4)

ȝierela (~n) *m.* garment (2)

ȝiernan *I* yearn for; entreat (228)

ȝierran (ȝear, gurron, o) *3* creak (1)

ȝierwan *I* make ready, prepare; dress; decorate (225)

ȝiest/gæst (~as) *m.* visitor, guest; stranger, enemy (51)

~líć *aj.* hospitable; terrible, strange (?) (322)

~líþ-ness *f.sg.* hospitality (68)

ȝiet(a) *av.* yet, still (93)

-ȝietan (ea, éa, ie) *5* acquire, get: be~ acquire, get: for~ forget: ofer~ forget: on~ understand (166)

ȝietan *I* make (blood) flow; destroy, kill (42)

ȝifer (~as) *m.* glutton (36)

ȝifre *aj.* useful (3)

ȝifre *aj.* greedy (36)

ȝift (~a; ~) *f.n.* gift; dowry (396)

ȝígant (~as) *m.* giant (3)

ȝimm (~as) *m.* gem-stone, jewel (32)

ȝimme(?)-ríce *n.sg.* splendid kingdom (486)

ȝin *n.sg.* vastness, abyss (21)

-ȝínan (-gán, -ȝinon, i) *1* gape: be~ swallow: to~ yawn, gape (21)

ȝinn *aj.* spacious (21)

~fæst *aj.* sample, liberal (372)

~wísed *aj.* of wide knowledge (?); of noble manners (?) (764; 10)

-ȝinnan (-gann, u, u) *3* begin: be~ begin: on~ begin, undertake, attempt; attack (236)

ȝíow/ȝíw *m.sg.* vulture (21)

ȝiren *see* grin

ȝísl (~as) *m.* hostage (2)

ȝítsere (ȝítseras) *m.* avaricious person (13)

ȝítsian *II* desire, covet (13)

ȝítsung (~a) *f.* avarice; lust (13)

glád *see* glídan

gladian *II* glitter, shine (39)

gléam *m.n.sg.* noisy revelry (7)

gléaw *aj.* clever, knowing, keen, wise; good (107)

gléawe *av.* wisely; well (107)

glemm (~as) *m.* wound (1)

for-glendran *I* devour (1)

glenǵ (~a) *f.* ornament; honor (9)

glenǵan *I* ornament, adorn (9)

gléo/glíeʒ (~) *n.* joy, music (16)

~stæf (-stafas) *m.* joy (40)

glida (~n) *m.* kite, vulture (24)

glídan (á, i, i) *1* glide, move, pass over, pass through: be~ glide away, disappear (24)

glíeʒ *see* gléo

glíewian *II* rejoice (16)

gliomu (glioma) *f.* splendor (1)

glitenian *II* glisten, shine (1)

glóf (~a) *f.* "glove," game-bag (2)

glóm *m.sg.* darkness, twilight (4)

glǽd *n.sg.* joy, gladness: *aj.* brilliant, radiant; happy, glad; gracious, kind (39)

glǽm *m.sg.* brilliance, beauty (1)

glæs *n.sg.* glass (3)

glœd (~a) *f.* glowing ember, coal (22)

glœdan *I* kindle, make hot (22)

gnagan (ó, ó, a) *6* gnaw (2)

gnást (~as) *m.* spark (1)

gnéaþ *aj.* stingy (2)

gnorn (~as) *m.* sorrow, grief, trouble (43)

~scyndende *ppl.aj.* hastening away in grief (9)

gnornian *II* grieve (43)

gnornung (~a) *f.* grief, lamentation (43)

gnyrn (~a) *f.* sorrow, grief, trouble (43)

gnætt (~as) *m.* gnat (1)

god (~as; ~u) *m.n.* (pagan) god; (Christian) God (1111)

~cund *aj.* divine (544)

~dóend, -dónd (-dœnd) *m.* benefactor (530)

~dréam (~as) *m.* celestial joy (149)

~spell (~) *n.* gospel (66)

~spellian *II* declare the gospel (66)

~webb (~) *n.* fine purple cloth (16)

gód (~) *n.* the good, goodness, virtue; goods, wealth; advantage, benefit (401)

gód (betera, sœlra; betst, sœlest) *aj.* good (better, best) (401)

gódian *II* do good; get better, improve; enrich (401)

gól *see* galan

gold (~) *n.* gold (185)

~hwæt *aj.* rich in gold (?); gold-bestowing (?); made of haunted gold (?) (47)

golden *see* ʒieldan

gollen *see* ʒiellan

golpen *see* ʒielpan

góma (~n) *m.* inside of the mouth, palate, jaws (13)

góp *m.sg.* servant, slave (?) (1)

gor *n.sg.* dirt, dung (1)

gós (gœs) *f.* goose (2)

goten *see* ʒéotan

gráf (~as) *m.* grove (1)

grafan (ó, ó, a) *6* dig; carve; engrave: á~ sculpt: be~ bury (17)

gram, ~e *aj.av.* cruel(ly), fierce(ly) (151)

gramm *see* grimman

grand *see* grindan

grandor-léas *aj.* guileless (1)

gránian *II* groan (1)

gráp (~a) *f.* grip, grasp (58)

gráp *see* grípan

grápian *II* grasp (58)

gréat *aj.* great, thick, stout (1)

gremian *II* enrage (151)

grennian *II* grin, grimace (2)

gréot (~) *n.* grit, sand, earth, dust (17)

gréotan (éa, u, o) *2* lament, weep (5)

griffus *m.sg.* griffin (1)

gríma (~n) *m.* mask, visor; specter (11)

grimm, ~e *aj.av.* fierce(ly), wild(ly) (151)

grimman (a, u, u) *3* rage, roar; become excited (?) (151)

grĭn/ʒiren *f.n.sg.* snare, noose (10)

ʒe-grind (~) *n.* crashing, commotion (15)

grindan (a, u, u) *3* grind (15)

grindel (grindlas) *m.* bar, bolt (1)

grípan (á, i, i) *1* grip, grasp (58)

gripe (∼) *m.* grip, grasp (58)

gripu (gripa) *f.* kettle, cauldron (58)

grist-bitian *II* gnash the teeth (97)

grist-bitung (∼a) *f.* gnashing of teeth (97)

griþ *n.sg.* truce, peace (1)

gróf *see* grafan

grorn, ∼e, *aj.av.* troubled, sad; sadly (6)

grornian *II* mourn (6)

grot (∼n) *n.* grain, particle (17)

grówan (éo, éo, ó) *7* grow, increase, spring up (18)

grum (?) *aj.* cruel, fierce (151)

grummon *see* grimman

grund (∼as) *m.* ground; abyss; bottom (of a body of water) (124)

grundon *see* grindan

grymettan *I* roar (151)

gryn/gyrn *m.f.n.* sorrow; harm (27)

gryndan *I* sink to the ground (124)

grynde (∼) *n.* abyss (124)

gryre (∼) *m.* terror (30)

grǽd (∼as) *m.* hunger; greed (17)

∼iʒ *aj.* greedy; eager, desirous (17)

grǽdan *I* cry out (1)

grǽf (grafu) *n.* grave (17)

grǽft (∼as) *m.* graven image (?) (17)

grǽʒ *aj.* gray (8)

grǽs *see* gærs

grœne *aj.* green (36)

grœnian *II* become green (36)

grœtan *I* greet, salute, speak to; approach, attack; touch (45)

guldon *see* ʒieldan

gullon *see* ʒiellan

-gunnon *see* -ʒinnan

gulpon *see* ʒielpan

guma (∼n) *m.* man (152)

gum-cyst (∼a) *f.* bravery, liberality, virtue (173)

gurron *see* ʒierran

guton *see* ʒéotan

gúþ (gúða) *f.* battle, fight, war (173)

∼mód *n.pl.(?)aj.(?)* warriors' hearts, courageous spirits (?); fierce-hearted, of warlike mind (?) (840)

∼wudu *m.sg.* spear (90)

gyden (∼a) *f.* goddess (1111)

gylden *aj.* made of gold, gilded (185)

gylt (∼as) *m.* guilt (21)

∼iʒ *aj.* guilty (21)

á-gyltan *I* sin, be guilty (21)

gyrdan *I* gird, bind round (42)

gyrdels (∼as) *m.* belt (42)

gyrn *see* gryn

gyrn-stæf (-stafas) *m.* tribulation (40)

gyte *m.sg.* flow; shedding (of blood) (42)

∼sæl *m.sg.* joy in drink-pouring (86)

gǽd *n.sg.* company, society (86)

∼eling (∼as) *m.* relative, companion (86)

gǽd *see* gád

gǽlan *I* hesitate, delay, hinder (8)

gǽlsa (∼n) *m.* pride, wantonness (38)

gǽrs/grǽs *n.sg.* grass (14)

gǽsne *aj.* barren, destitute; dead (9)

gǽst *see* ʒiest

gǽst/gást (∼as) *m.* ghost, soul, spirit; angel; demon, devil (408)

∼líć, ∼e *aj.av.* spiritual, ghostly, spiritually, in spirit; frightful (322)

gǽstan *I* frighten; torment; persecute (2)

H

habban (hæfde) *III* have, hold, possess, keep: be∼ comprehend; surround: for∼ hold back, restrain oneself; prevent: ʒe∼ hold fast: wiðer∼ withstand (771)

hád (∼as) *m.* state, condition, rank, order; nature, form; person, individual; sex: *suff.* -hood (60)

hádor *n.sg.* brightness (13)

hádor/hǽdre *aj.* bright, clear; clear-voiced (13)

hádre/hǽdre *av.* brightly, clearly (13)

hafenian *II* hold firmly, hold up, lift (771)

hafoc (~as) *m.* hawk, falcon (8)

hafola (~n) *m.* head (16)

haga (~n) *m.* enclosure, hedge; dwelling (22)

hagol/hæʒ(e)1 (hæʒelas) *m.* sleet, hailstone, hail; name of H-rune (16)

hagu-steald (~as) *m.* young unmarried man, young warrior: *n.sg.* celibacy: *aj.* bachelor, young (13)

hál *aj.* whole, healthy, intact (272)

~iʒ *aj.* holy: *as sb.* (~e) *m.* saint: ~monaþ *m.sg.* September (597)

~wende *aj.* healing, salutary (213)

hálgian *II* make holy, hallow (597)

hálgung *f.sg.* consecration, hallowing (597)

hálor *see* hǽl

háls *f.sg.* salvation (272)

hálsung (~a) *f.* supplication (272)

hám (~as) *m.* dwelling, manor, home (240)

ham(a) (~as; ~n) *m.* coat, covering (93)

hama *aj.* coated, furnished with a coat (93)

hamelian *II* hamstring (1)

hamor (~as) *m.* hammer (7)

hana (~n) *m.* cock (4)

han-crǽd *m.sg.* cock-crow (4)

hand (~a) *f.* hand (310)

~ʒe-sella (~n) *m.* companion (142)

~ʒe-weorc (~) *n.* handiwork; creation (538)

~hrine *m.sg.* touch (27)

~locen *ppl.aj.* linked by hand (117)

ʒe-hang (~) *n.* hanging(s), appendage, limb (46)

hangelle (hangellan) *f.* a hanging object (46)

hangen *see* hón

hangian *II(intr.)* hang (46)

hár *aj.* hoary, grey, old (30)

hás *aj.* hoarse (1)

hasu/haswiʒ *aj.* dark, dusky (9)

hát (~) *n.* heat (96)

hát ~e *aj.av.* hot, burning, intense, passionate, inspiring; hotly, fiercely (96)

~wende *aj.* hot, burning (213)

ʒe-hát (~) *n.* promise, vow (332)

hata (~n) *m.* enemy (75)

hátan (hét/heht, é, á) 7 call, name, promise, command: ~, hátte *pres.-pret.sg.* be called, named: ʒe~ promise, threaten (332)

hatian *II* hate (75)

háwe *aj.* visible (1)

héa- *pref.* high: *cp.* héah- (492)

~líc *aj.* high; eminent; arrogant: ~e *av.* highly, remarkably (322)

heaðor *n.sg.* enclosure (5)

heaðorian *II* shut in, confine (5)

heaðu- *pref.* battle-, warlike (66)

héaf *m.sg.* grief, lamentation (21)

be-héafdian *II* behead (99)

héafod (héafdas; héafod; héafdu) *m.n.* head: *pref.* chief (99)

héah (híerra, híehst) *aj.* high, tall, lofty; great, exalted, illustrious; profound; proud, arrogant: *pref.* ~, héa- (492)

héah (héar, híehst) *av.* high (492)

heald *aj.* bent, prone (26)

-heald *suff.* sloping, inclining (26)

ʒe-heald *n.sg.* custody, keeping (443)

healdan (éo, éo, ea) 7 hold, keep, occupy, possess, rule; observe; defend, preserve: for~ disregard, rebel against (443)

healdend *m.sg.* guardian, protector, ruler; God (443)

healf (~a) *f.* half, side (55)

healf *aj.* half (55)

heall (~a) *f.* hall, common-room, residence (41)

healm (~as) *m.* straw (1)

healp *see* helpan

heals (~as) *m.* neck; prow (of a ship) (109)

~fæst *aj.* arrogant, obstinate (372)

~ʒe-bedda (~n) *m.f.* beloved bed-fellow, consort (33)

~mæȝeþ (~) *f.* beloved maiden (54)

healsian *II* entreat, implore (109)

healsre-feðer *f.sg.* pillow down (56)

healt *aj.* lame, halt (3)

héan, ~e *aj.av.* low(ly), abject(ly), poor(ly), vile(ly) (92)

héap (~as) *m.* crowd, band, troop, heap (56)

heard *n.sg.* what is hard: *aj.* hard, strong, brave; constant; hard, cruel, obstinate; difficult (?): ~e *av.* cruelly, grievously; tightly, closely; with difficulty; exceedingly (261)

~ing (~as) *m.* bold man (261)

~rǽd *aj.* constant, resolute (174)

hearg (~as; ~e) *m.f.* (pagan) temple, fane; grove, forest (72)

hearm (~as) *m.* harm, affliction, grief; evil, calumny, insult: *aj.* harmful, evil (53)

~scearu *f.sg.* affliction (52)

~stæf (-stafas) *m.* harm, sorrow (40)

hearpe (hearpan) *f.* harp (22)

hearpere (hearperas) *m.* harpist (22)

hearra (~n) *m.* lord, master (32)

ȝe-héaw *n.sg.* grinding (1)

héawan (éo, éo, éa) *7* hew, cut down, kill (19)

hebban (hóf, ó, æ) *I-6* raise, lift (139)

hefiȝ *aj.av.* heavy, severe; heavily, gravely (33)

hefiȝian *II* weigh down upon, afflict; (*intr.*) become heavy, weakened (33)

heht *see* hátan

helan (æ, ǽ, o) *4* conceal, hide, cover (164)

be-helian *I* bury, hide (164)

hell *f.sg.* hell: hell(e)- *pref.* hellish, infernal (164)

~heoðu *f.sg.* chamber of hell (?) (1)

~rúne (-rúnan) *f.* hellish magician, demon(ess) (78)

helm (~as) *m.* protector; protection, covering, helmet; crown (164)

helm(i)an *I-II* cover (164)

help *f.sg.* help (100)

helpan (ea, u, o) *3* help (100)

helpend (~) *m.* helper (100)

hemman *I* close up, shut up (1)

hendan *I* hold (310)

ȝe-hende *aj.av.* at hand, near to (310)

héng *see* hón

ȝe-henȝe *aj.* having an inclination to, inclined to (46)

henȝest (~as) *m.* stallion, steed (13)

henn/hæn *f.sg.* hen (4)

hentan *I* pursue; seize (2)

héofan (héofde/héof, héofon *as if from* héafan) *I-7* lament, grieve (21)

heofon, ~e (~as; heofonan) *m.f.* heaven, the heavens, sky (542)

~cund *aj.* coming from heaven, celestial (55)

héofung (~a) *f.* lamentation (21)

héold *see* healdan

heolfor *n.sg.* (clotted) blood (12)

heolfriȝ *aj.* bloody (12)

heoloþ- *pref.* concealing, of concealment (164)

~cynn *n.sg.* tribe of hell (389)

~helm *m.sg.* helmet of invisibility (164)

heolstor (heolstras) *m.* hiding place, darkness: *aj.* dark (164)

heorcnian/hyrcnian *II* hear, harken (2)

heord *m.sg.* hair (1)

heord (~a) *f.* custody; herd, flock; family (71)

heorot (~as) *m.* hart, stag (5)

heorr (~as) *m.* hinge (1)

ȝe-heort *aj.* courageous (242)

-heort *suff.* -hearted (242)

heorte (heortan) *f.* heart (242)

heort-léas *aj.* dispirited (224)

heoru *m.sg.* sword: *pref.* sword-, battle-, death-, *etc.* (44)

~swealwe *f.sg.* falcon, hawk (1)

heorþ (heorðas) *m.* hearth; fire (13)

héow *see* héawan

héoþ *f.sg.* interior of a hall (2)

hér *av.* here (280)

here (herȝas) *m.* armed force, multitude (63)

here-líć *aj.* praiseworthy (153)

here-ness *f.sg.* praise (153)

hergian *II* harry, lay waste (63)

herian *I* praise, honor (153)

hét *see* hátan

hete *m.sg.* hatred, hate (75)

hetlen *aj.* hostile (75)

hettend (∼; ∼e) *m.* enemy (75)

híce *f.sg.* frog (1)

hider *av.* hither (49)

híeȝ *n.sg.* hay (8)

híe(ȝ)an *I* exalt; worship (492)

híeȝan *I* hold (a meeting); perform, keep (a fast); carry out, achieve (12)

híehst *see* héah

híehþu (híehþa) *f.* height (492)

hield (∼a) *f.* keeping, protection, grace (443)

ȝe-hield *n.sg.* keeping, custody; secret place (443)

hieldan *I* incline, bend, bow, descend; incline, force downwards, lay down (26)

á-hieltan *I* trip up (3)

híenan *I* lower, abase, humiliate (92)

híenþ(u) (híenþa) *f.* humiliation (92)

híeran *I* hear; obey; serve: ofer∼ disobey (296)

hierdan *I* make bold, make hard (261)

hierde (hierdas) *m.* herder, shepherd, guardian (71)

hierd-ness *f.sg.* custody, watch (71)

híere *aj.* pleasant, mild; pure (19)

hier-ness *f.sg.* hearing (296)

híerra *see* héah, *aj.*

ȝe-hierstan *I* roast (1)

híer-sum *aj.* obedient (296)

hiertan *I* hearten, encourage (242)

hierwan (hierede/hierwede) *I* mistreat; condemn, despise; blaspheme (9)

híew (∼) *n.* form, color (26)

híewe *aj.* colored, beautiful (26)

ȝe-híewian *II* form, give shape to (26)

hígian *II* hasten, strive: ofer∼ overpower, get the better of (2)

higore/higere *f.sg.* jay, magpie (1)

hild (∼a) *f.* battle, warfare: hilde- *pref.* of battle, warlike (155)

hilt (∼as) *m.* sword-hilt, pommel (11)

∼ed *aj.* furnished with a hilt, hilted (11)

ȝe-hilte (∼) *f.n.* sword-hilt, pommel (11)

hin- *pref.* away (65)

hinan *see* hionan

hinca (∼n) *m.* one who is lame (1)

hind (∼a) *f.* hind, doe (1)

hindan *av.* from behind (30)

∼weard *av.* at the end (882)

hindema *aj.* hindmost (30)

hinder *av.* back, after (30)

∼hóc *m.sg.* trick, snare (2)

∼ling *av.* backwards (30)

∼weard *aj.* backward, slow (882)

hinde-weardere *m.sg.* attendant at the rear (257)

hío-dæȝ *av.* today (502)

hiona(n), hionane *av.* from here, hence (65)

híred *m.sg.* household, group of retainers, company (14)

hitt *f.sg.* heat (96)

híwan *m.pl.* members of a family or (lay or monastic) household (14)

to-hlacan (6, ó, a) *6* disband, disperse (?) (1)

hlacor (?) *aj.* screaming (?) (1)

hlád *see* hlídan

hladan (ó, ó, a) *6* load, pile up; lay; furnish, adorn; draw: á∼ draw out, lead forth (24)

-hladen *ppl.suff.* -laden, -adorned (24)

hláf (∼as) *m.* loaf, bread (89)

∼mæsse *f.sg.* Lammas (August 1st) (6)

hláford (∼as) *m.* lord, master (89)

hlamm *see* hlimman

hlanc *aj.* lank, thin (2)

hláw *see* hlǽw

hleahtor *m.sg.* noise; laughter; jubilation; scorn (32)

hléapan (éo, éo, éa) *7* run, jump, leap: ȝe~ mount (a horse) (15)

hléat *see* hléotan

hlemm (~as) *m.* sound, noise (15)

hlemman *I* sound noisily (15)

hlenće (hlenćan) *f.* armor (1)

hléoðor (~) *n.* voice, sound, song; hearing; prophecy (62)

hléoðrian *II* speak, sound out, resound (of the voice) (62)

hléonaþ *m.sg.* shelter (61)

hléop *see* hléapan

hléor (~) *n.* cheek, face (22)

~beorg *f.sg.* cheek-protector, helmet (?): ~beran *f.pl.* cheek-guard, helmet (?) (398; 652)

~dropa (~n) *m.* tear (9)

hléotan (éa, u, o) *2* cast lots; obtain (by lot), have fall one's lot (20)

hléow *m.sg.* protection; protector (61)

~lora *m.sg.* one without a protector (224)

~stól *m.sg.* shelter, asylum (51)

hléowian *II* protect, cherish; warm (61)

hlid (~u) *n.* lid, covering, roof; door, gate (16)

hlídan (á, i, i) *1* close, cover: be~ close: on~ open, reveal; appear: to~ open, split (16)

ȝe-hliðu *n.pl.* gates (32)

hliehhan (hlóg, ó, *def.*) *1-6* laugh, deride; rejoice (32)

hlíep (~as) *m.* leap, jump (15)

hlíet (~as) *m.* share, lot (20)

hlíewþ (~a) *f.* shelter, covering (61)

hlĭfian *II* tower, stand high (17)

hlígan (á, i, hliȝen) *1* attribute to (1)

hlimman (a, u, u) *3* resound, roar (15)

hlimme *f.sg.* stream, torrent (15)

hlin- *pref.* reclining, leaning; railed, grated (17)

~bedd *n.sg.* bed of rest, of death (33)

~duru *f.sg.* prison door (37)

~reced *n.sg.* prison (42)

~scu(w)a *m.sg.* darkness of prison (16)

hlinć (~as) *m.* hill (3)

hli(o)nian *II* incline, slope, rest (17)

hlísa *m.sg.* fame, repute (10)

hlĭþ (~; hliþu) *n.* slope, hillside (31)

hlód *see* hladan

hlóðian *II* despoil, plunder (13)

hlóg *see* hliehhan

hlosnian *II* listen (10)

hloten *see* hléotan

hlóþ (hlóða) *f.* troop, crowd (13)

hlúd, ~e *aj.av.* loud(ly) (63)

hlummon *see* hlimman

hluton *see* hléotan

hlútor, hlútre *aj.av.* bright(ly), clear(ly), pure(ly) (37)

hlúttrian *II* clean, purify (37)

Hlýda *m.sg.* March (63)

hlýdan *I* make a noise (63)

ȝe-hlýde *n.sg.* cry, clamor (63)

hlyne *f.sg.* maple-tree (1)

hlynn *m.sg.* noise (15)

ȝe-hlynn *n.sg.* noise (15)

hlynnan *I* resound; shout (15)

hlynsian *II* resound (15)

hlyst *f.sg.* listening, hearing (10)

hlystan *I* listen to (10)

hlytm (~as) *m.* cast of lots (20)

hlǽder (hlǽdra) *f.* ladder (4)

hlǽf-díȝe (-dígan) *f.* lady of the house, mistress (89)

ȝe-hlǽȝ *n.sg.* derision (32)

hlǽnan *I* cause to lean: á~ set oneself up: be~ set around (17)

hlǽst (~) *n.* burden (5)

ȝe-hlǽstan *I* weigh down, load; adorn (5)

hlǽw/hláw (~as) *m.* cave; hill; barrow, tumulus, mound (10)

ȝe-hlœ́ða (~n) *m.* companion (13)

be-hlœ́ðan *I* despoil, plunder (13)

hnág *aj.* abject, mean, humble; humiliating (30)

hnág *see* hnígan

hnappian *II* doze, nap (2)

hnappung (~a) *f.* napping, sleeping (2)

ȝe-hnást *n.sg.* clash (7)

á-hnéap *see* á-hnéopan

hnéaw *aj.* niggardly (5)

hnecca (~n) *m.* neck (1)

á-hnéopan (éa, u, o) *2* pick, pluck (1)

hnesce *aj.* soft (4)

hnígan (á, i, hniȝen) *1* bow down, bend low (30)

hnipian *II* bend, bow the head (1)

hnítan (á, i, i) *1* clash (7)

hnossian *II* strike (2)

ȝe-hnyst *aj.* contrite (2)

ȝe-hnǽćan *I* overthrow, destroy (1)

hnǽgan *I* bow down; humble, vanquish (30)

ȝe-hnǽst, -hnást *n.sg.* clash (7)

hóc *m.sg.* hook, barb (2)

~iht *aj.* hooked, barbed (2)

hoðma (~n) *m.* darkness, grave (2)

hof (~u) *n.* court, court-yard, apartment; dwelling; temple (51)

hóf (~as) *m.* hoof (1)

hóf *see* hebban

be-hófian *II* require (5)

hogian *II* think (571)

hóh (hós) *m.* hough, heel; promontory, headland (3)

hol (~u) *n.* hollow (in the ground): *aj.* hollow (5)

hól (~) *n.* vain speech (3)

ȝe-hola (~n) *m.* protector, defender (164)

hold *aj.av.* loyal, kind, friendly, gracious; devoutly, kindly (144)

holen *m.sg.* holly (2)

holen *see* helan

holm (~as) *m.* sea, ocean, wave, water (42)

~iȝ *aj.* pertaining to the sea (42)

holpen *see* helpan

holt (~) *n.* grove, copse, wood (32)

~wudu (-wuda) *m.* wood, forest; wooden shield (90)

hólunga *av.* in vain (3)

hón [<*hóhan <*hanhan] (héng, é, a) *7* (*tr.*) hang; crucify: á~ hang, crucify: be~, ȝe~ (*intr.*) hang (a thing) with (something) (46)

hop (~u) *n.* remote valley; hiding-place (3)

hóp (~as) *m.* wave (2)

~iȝ *aj.* eddying, surging (2)

hopa (~n) *m.* hope (3)

hopian *II* hope, expect (3)

hoppa (~n) *m.* hopper (2)

hoppettan *I* jump, hop, leap (2)

hord (~) *n.* hoard, treasure, treasury (106)

horh (hóras) *m.* phlegm, mucus; filth (4)

horn (~as) *m.* (beast's, drinking, musical) horn; projection, gable (of a building), prow (of a ship) (36)

hors (~) *n.* horse (8)

horsc *aj.* lively; wise (9)

hós *f.sg.* troop, company (2)

hosp *m.sg.* rebuke, insult, blasphemy (12)

hrace (hracan) *f.* throat, gorge (2)

hran (~as) *m.* whale (9)

hrán *see* hrínan

hrand *see* hrindan

hrang *see* hringan

hráw *see* hrǽw

hréad *see* hréodan

-hréad *suff.* clothed, adorned (46)

hréam (~as) *m.* cry, alarm (5)

hréas *see* hréosan

hréaw *see* hréowan

hreddan *I* save, rescue (18)

hreðer (~as) *m.* breast, heart (52)

hréodan (éa, u, o) *2* adorn, ornament (46)

hréoða (~n) *m.* covering, protection (46)

hréof *aj.* rough, scabby, leprous (3)

hréoh *n.sg.* stormy weather (30)

hréoh/hréow *aj.* rough, angry, fierce; stormy; troubled, sad (30)

hréop *see* hrópan

hréoriȝ *aj.* in ruins (50)

hréosan (éa, hruron, o) *2* fall, fall down, go to ruin: be∼ fall upon; cover (50)

hréow (∼a) *f.* sorrow, regret: *aj.*: see hréoh (24)

hréowan (éa, éa, éo) *7* grieve, grieve for; regret (15)

hrepp(i)an *I-II* touch (3)

hríðiȝ *aj.* storm-beaten (2)

hrif (∼u) *n.* belly, womb (7)

hrím *m.sg.* hoar-frost, rime (17)

∼iȝ *aj.* covered with hoar-frost (17)

hrímde (?) *ppl. aj.* frosted (17)

be-hríman *I* cover with hoar-frost (17)

hrínan (á, i, i) *1* touch, reach (27)

hrindan (a, i, i) *3* thrust (1)

hrinde *ppl.aj.* frosted (17)

hring (∼as) *m.* ring; twisted ornament; armor of interlocked rings; fetter (65)

∼boga *m.sg.* coiled being, dragon (172)

∼ed *aj.* made of interlocked rings (65)

∼mere *n.sg.* circular pool, bath (84)

∼mǽl *m.sg.* ring-hilted or ring-marked sword: ∼ed *aj.* hilted or marked with rings (72)

∼sele *m.sg.* hall of generosity: treasure-chamber (of a dragon's lair) (142)

hring (∼as) *m.* ringing, sound (65)

hringan (a, u, u) *3* ring out, sound (65)

hrísel *f.*(?)*sg.* shuttle of a loom (2)

hrissan *I* shake, rattle (2)

hríþ (hríða) *f.* snowstorm (2)

hroden *see* hréodan

hróðor (hróðras) *m.* joy; benefit (137)

hróf (∼as) *m.* roof, covering (44)

hrópan (éo, éo, ó) *7* cry out; proclaim (8)

hrór *aj.* active; brave, strong (43)

hroren *see* hréosan

hróst-béag *m.sg.* supporting wood-work (of a roof) (172)

hrudon *see* hréodan

hrung (∼a) *f.* rung, spoke, bar (1)

hrungon *see* hringan

hruron *see* hréosan

hrúse (hrúsan) *f.* earth (as material) (45)

hrútan (éa, u, o) *2* roar (1)

hrycg (∼as) *m.* back, spine; surface, crest of a sea (14)

hryre *m.sg.* fall, downfall, death, calamity (50)

hræd *aj.* quick, ready, active (128)

(h)ræðe *aj.av.* quick(ly) (128)

hræfn (∼as) *m.* raven (20)

hræȝl (∼) *n.* garment (33)

hrǽw/hráw (∼) *n.* body; corpse (20)

hrœ́ðan *I* glory, exult (137)

(h)rœ́ðe *aj.av.* angry, cruel, fierce; harshly, fiercely (50)

ȝe-hrœ́fan *I* roof (44)

hrœ́man *I* exult, exult in (21)

hrœ́miȝ *aj.* exultant; clamorous (21)

hrœ́ran *I* move, stir, disturb (43)

hrœ́r-ness (∼a) *f.* disturbance (43)

hrœ́þ *n.sg.* fame, glory (137)

hú *av.* how (242)

∼líc *pron.* what kind of (322)

hulpon *see* helpan

hund (∼as) *m.* dog (60)

hund *num.* hundred: *pref.* decade: ∼ni-gun-tiȝ 90: ∼red 100: ∼siofun-tiȝ 70: ∼téon-tiȝ 100: ∼twelf-tiȝ 120 (60)

huneȝ *m.sg.* honey (8)

hungor *m.sg.* hunger (41)

hungriȝ *aj.* hungry (41)

hunta (∼n) *m.* huntsman (3)

huntoþ *m.sg.* hunting (3)

hup-seax (∼) *n.* hip-sword, short sword (9)

húru *av.* at least, indeed, certainly, even, yet (62)

hús (∼) *n.* building, group of buildings, house; household, family, race (112)

husc *n.sg.* mockery, scorn (6)

Húsel (∼) *n.* Eucharist, the Host (5)

∼fæt (-fatu) *n.* sacramental vessel (31)

húþ (húðа) *f.* booty, objects of booty (25)

hwá *pron.* who, anyone, someone (521)

ȝe-hwá *pron.* each one, anyone, whoever (521)

hwam (∼as) *m.* corner (4)

hwám/hwǽm *pron.dat.*, *see* hwá, hwæt (521)

hwanan *av.* whence, from where (11)

hwanne *see* hwænne

hwealf (∼a) *f.* arch, vaulting: *aj.* hollow (8)

hwealfan *I* cover, vault over (8)

hwearf (∼as) *m.* crowd, troop; wharf, shore (207)

∼líć (?) *aj.* active (?); obedient (?); short-lived, mortal (?) (322)

hwearf *see* hweorfan

hwearfian *II* revolve (207)

hwearft (∼as) *m.* circuit (207)

hwelan (æ, ǽ, o) *4* roar, rage (2)

hwelć/hwilć *pron.* which, what; whichever, any (one), each: ȝe∼ each, any, many, all, whatever (477)

hwelp (∼as) *m.* whelp, cub (4)

hwéol (∼) *n.* wheel (5)

hwéop *see* hwópan

hweorf *aj.* clever, practised (207)

hweorfan (ea, u, o) *3* turn, return, change, move about, go: á∼ (*tr.*, *intr.*) turn away, turn aside: and∼ go against, turn against: be∼ turn, change: ȝe∼ (*tr.*) turn, convert; (*intr.*) turn, go away, pass: ȝeond∼ pass through, go about: on∼ (*tr.*) change, reverse; (*intr.*) change, revert: to∼ part, scatter: ymb(e)∼ move around, circle: æt∼ go, turn (207)

hwer *m.sg.* pot, kettle (1)

hwerȝen *av.* somewhere (136)

hwettan *I* incite, rouse: á∼ excite; bestow; reject, drive away with a curse (47)

hwí/hwý *av.cj.* why (521)

hwider *av.* whither, where: ȝe∼ everywhere (9)

hwiðu *f.sg.* air, breeze (1)

be-hwielfan *I* cover, vault over (1)

hwierfan *I* turn; convert, be converted; revolve, move about, be whirled: á∼ turn away: be∼ move around: for∼ transform, pervert: ȝe∼ turn away, convert, pervert, change: ymb∼ move around (207)

hwíl (∼a) *f.* while, period, time; a long time (206)

∼wende *aj.* transitory, temporal (213)

hwilć *see* hwelć

hwíle *av.* once, for a time (206)

hwílen *aj.* transitory, passing (206)

hwilpe (hwilpan) *f.* a water-bird (1)

hwílum *av.dat.* at times, now and then (206)

hwínan (á, i, i) *1* hiss, whistle (1)

hwít *aj.* white, luminous, shining, splendid (32)

∼locc, -locced *aj.* fair-haired, with shining hair (117)

hwítan *I* whiten; polish (?) (32)

hwón *aj.av.* a little, a few; somewhat (13)

hwópan (éo, éo, ó) *7* threaten (6)

hworfen *see* hweorfan

hwurfon *see* hweorfan

hwý *see* hwí

hwyrft (∼as) *m.* circuit, course; outlet (207)

hwæðer *pron.* which of two; whichever: *cj.* whether (186)

hwæðere *av.* however, yet, anyhow: ȝe∼ however, nevertheless (186)

hwæl (hwalas) *m.* whale (11)

hwælen *aj.* like a whale (11)

hwǽlon *see* hwelan

hwǽm/hwám *dat.sg.*, *see* hwá, hwæt

hwænne/hwanne *av.cj.* when; until (27)

hwǽr *av.* where: ȝe∼ anywhere, everywhere (136)

hwæt *pron.* what (521)

∼hwega *av.* a little, sometimes (521)

hwæt *aj.* sharp, keen, quick, valiant (47)

~ræd *aj.* determined, resolute (174)

hwæt *interj.av.* what, indeed, truly, behold, lo, thus (521)

hwæt(e) *m.* wheat, corn (5)

hwæten *aj.* wheaten (5)

hwǿne *av.* somewhat, a little (13)

hycgan (hogde/hogode) *III* think, consider; intend, hope: á~ think out, devise, invent: be~ be concerned about: for~ despise, reject: ʒe~ think, consider, resolve, determine; hope: ofer~ despise, scorn: on~ consider: wiþ~ despise, scorn (571)

hycgende *ppl.suff.* -thinking, -minded (571)

hýd (~a) *f.* hide, skin (2)

hýdan *I* hide, conceal (34)

ʒe-hýdan *I* make fast with a hide cable (?) (2)

hýðan *I* plunder, take booty (25)

hýðe-líc *aj.* fitting, proper, pleasing (3)

hyʒd (~u) *f.n.* mind, thought (571)

~iʒ *aj.* mindful: *suff.* -minded (571)

hyʒe (~) *m.* mind, heart, soul; thought, purpose (571)

~gælsa *aj.* hesitant, sluggish (8)

~léast *f.sg.* folly (224)

~scæft (~a) *f.* heart, mind (340)

hyht (~e) *m.* hope, intent; joy (128)

hyhtan *I* hope, trust; hope for; exult, rejoice (128)

hyldu *f.sg.* kindness, favor, friendship, loyalty (144)

hyll (~as) *m.* hill (5)

hylman *I* cover, conceal: for~ neglect, refuse obedience to: ofer~ prevaricate (164)

hyngran *I* be hungry (41)

hype (hypas) *m.* hip (3)

hýr (~a) *f.* hire, pay (2)

hýra (~n) *m.* servant (2)

hyrcnian *see* heorcnian

hyrd *f.sg.* door (1)

on-hyrian *I* imitate (2)

hyrned *aj.* horned, beaked (36)

hyrst (~as) *m.* hurst; wood (1)

hyrst (~a) *f.* ornament, equipment (46)

hyrstan *I* decorate, equip (46)

on-hyscan *I* abominate (6)

hyse (hyssas) *m.* young man (24)

~beorðor *n.sg.* young man (652)

hyspan *I* mock, scorn (12)

hýþ (hýða) *f.* landing place, harbor (10)

hæbbende *ppl.suff.* -having, -bearing(771)

hædre *av.* anxiously (60)

hædre *see* hádor, hádre

hǽðen *aj.* heathen, pagan (68)

hæf (hafu) *n.* sea (9)

hæfen *see* hebban

hæft (~as) *m.* bond, fetter; captive (62)

~ling (~as) *m.* prisoner (62)

hæft (~) *n.* handle, hilt (62)

hæfta (~n) *m.* prisoner (62)

hæftan *I* fetter, capture (62)

hæftnian *II* take prisoner (62)

ʒe-hæʒ *n.sg.* enclosure; meadow (22)

ʒe-hǽʒan *I* torment (?) (1)

hæʒ(e)l *see* hagol

hæʒ-steald *aj.* young (14)

hæl *see* helan

hǽl (*dat.sg.* hálor) *n.* well-being, safety, salvation, good fortune; omen(s) (272)

hǽlan *I* make whole, heal (272)

hæle (hæleðas) *m.* warrior, man (239)

Hǽlend *m.sg.* the Healer, Saviour (272)

hæleþ (~) *m.* warrior, man (239)

hǽlsian *II* salute, greet (272)

hǽlu *f.sg.* well-being; salvation (272)

hǽman *I* marry; cohabit with (240)

hǽmed *n.sg.* marriage; cohabitation (240)

hæn *see* henn

hǽr (~) *n.* hair (6)

hærfest *m.sg.* harvest season (7)

hærn (~a) *f.* wave, sea (2)

hǽs (~e) *f.* order, command (15)

hǽst (~a) *f.* violence (7)

hǽste *aj.* violently (7)

on-hǽtan *I* heat (96)

hætt *m.sg.* hat, *tribal name* Hættware (2)

hættian *II* scalp, "remove the hat" (2)

hǽtu *f.sg.* heat (96)

hǽwen *aj.* blue-green-gray (1)

hǽþ *m.n.sg.* heath, open level wasteland (68)

hœ́dan *I* protect, heed, attend to (8)

hœ́la (~n) *m.* heel, track, footstep (1)

I

ić, þú, hé, etc. *pers.poss.pron.* (15974)

icge *aj.(?)av.(?)* glorious (?); eagerly (?) (1)

ídel *aj.* vacant, empty; deprived of (39)

~hende *aj.* empty-handed (310)

~ness (~a) *f.* frivolity, vanity (39)

ides (~a) *f.* lady, woman (64)

ídiȝ *aj.* busy, active (?); greedy for (?) (1)

ídlian *II* become empty, useless (39)

íećan (íehte/íecte) *I* increase, add to (375)

íeðan *I* devastate, lay waste (5)

ȝe-íeðan *I* alleviate (141)

íeðe *aj.* easy, agreeable, pleasant, smooth (141)

íeðe *aj.* waste, empty (5)

íeðe *see* éaðe

íeðring (?) *f.sg.* alleviation, relief (?) (141)

íeȝ (~a) *f.* island, watered land (25)

~land (~) *n.* island (231)

ieldan *I* delay: for~ defer, postpone (179)

ielde *m.pl.* human beings, men (179)

ielding *f.sg.* delay (179)

ieldra, ieldest *see* eald

ieldu (ielde) *f.* age, old age; *pl.* (the) years of one's life (179)

ielf (~e) *m.* elf (11)

ielfetu (ielfeta) *f.* swan (1)

ierfe (ierfu) *n.* inheritance (45)

~láf *f.sg.* heirloom; heir (78)

~weard *m.sg.* heir (257)

ierȝþu *f.sg.* slackness (10)

ierman *I* make miserable (169)

iermen *see* eormen

ierming (~as) *m.* poor wretch (169)

iermþu (iermþa) *f.* wretchedness, misery, poverty (169)

ierre *n.sg.* anger: *aj.* angry (113)

~þweorh (?) *aj.* very angry (?) (4)

ierrunga *av.* angrily (113)

iersian *II* be angry (113)

iersung (~a) *f.* anger (113)

íewan *I* show, present, reveal (82)

íeþ *see* éaðe

ílca *wk.aj.* (the) same (38)

in/on *prep.* in, on, into, upon; at, to, towards, among; during; in respect of (4747)

in/inn *av.* in, inside of, inwards (4747)

in-, inn- *pref.* in, into (*also as intensifier*) (4747)

inca (~n) *m.* offence, grievance (4)

~þeode (?) *f.pl.* hostile nation (460)

incge-láf *f.sg.* ancestral sword (?) (78)

Ing *m.sg.* eponymous god of the Ing-wine (Danes); name of NG-rune (3)

inn (~) *n.* chamber, dwelling, lodging (3)

inn *av.* inside, in, inwardly (4747)

inn- *pref.* in, into (*also as intensifier*) (4747)

~dryhten *aj.* very noble, distinguished (1268)

~dryhtu (-dryhta) *f.* honor, glory (1268)

~flœ́de *aj.* overflowing (122)

~fród *aj.* very old, wise (80)

~ȝeare *av.* altogether, completely (225)

~ȝe-folc (~) *n.* native race (430)

~genȝa *m.sg.* invader (264)

~ȝe-steald *n.sg.* domestic possessions (14)

~ȝe-þeode *f.pl.* native people (460)

~ȝíemend (~) *m.* native ruler (32)

~lende *aj.* native (231)

~líće *av.* inwardly, sincerely (322)

~stæpes *av.* directly, forthwith (39)

~weorod *n.sg.* household, retainers (220)

innan *av.* from within, within, inside (4747)

~cund *av.* coming from within (55)

~weard *aj.* directed to within, inner, interior (882)

inne *av.* inside, in, inwardly (4747)

~weard *aj.* directed to within, inner, interior (882)

innera *aj.* interior, inner (4747)

ʒe-innian *II* fill (4747)

innoþ *m.f.sg.* insides, interior, womb (4747)

intinga (~n) *m.* cause, matter (2)

inwidda (~) *m.* adversary, enemy (19)

inwitt *n.sg.* malice: *aj.* wicked, deceitful (19)

íoh *see* íw

íor (?) *m.sg.* eel (?); for Old Norse *jár "year" (?); name of early [j]- or yod-rune, later IO-rune (1)

iornan (ea, u, u) *3* run, pass by: á~ run out, pass by: be~ run into; incur; occur to: of~ hasten away from: on~ fly open, give way: to~ move widely about: þurh~ run through (41)

íren/íse(r)n (~) *n.* iron, sword (of low carbon steel): *aj.* iron, of iron (48)

ís *n.sg.* ice; name of I-rune (14)

~iʒ *aj.* icy; covered with ice (?) (14)

íse(r)n *see* íren

istoria *n.sg.* history (1)

íu *see* ʒéo

íw/íoh *m.sg.* yew-tree; name of ʒ- or yogh-rune (2)

L

lá *interj.* lo, indeed (19)

lác (~) *f.n.* movement, tumult; game, play, dance; fight; fate (?); gift, offering, sacrifice; booty (200)

ʒe-laca (~) *m.* warrior (200)

lácan (leolc, *def.*) *7* move, jump, dance; leap up, fly, swing; measure off;

fight: be~ enclose: for~ betray, deceive: ʒeond~ traverse (200)

-lácend *ppl.suff.* fighter, flyer (200)

lácnian *II* treat medically, cure (15)

lád (~a) *f.* journey, way, course; support (240)

ládian *II* excuse (3)

láðe *av.* hatefully, evilly (197)

laðian *II* invite (11)

á-láðian *II* become hateful (197)

laðu (laða) *f.* invitation, summons (11)

láf (~e) *f.* leavings, remnant, residue; survivor (78)

ʒe-lafian *II* refresh, lave (1)

lágon *see* licgan

lagu *m.sg.* sea, water; name of L-rune (54)

lagu (~a) *f.* law, order, command (5)

ʒe-lagu *n.pl.* extent, surface (of the sea) (54)

láh *see* líon

lám (~) *n.* loam, clay (13)

lama (~n) *m.* lame man: *aj.* lame (6)

lamb(or) (lambru) *n.* lamb (5)

lamp *see* limpan

land (~) *n.* land; earth, soil; territory, (native) country, realm (231)

~sciepe *m.sg.* region (340)

lang (lenǵra, lenǵest) *aj.* long, tall; lasting (286)

~ʒe-stréon (~) *n.* long-kept, ancient treasure (38)

~sum *aj.* long-lasting (137)

~twídiʒ *aj.* granted for a long time, long-lasting (1)

-lang *suff.* belonging to, dependent on, pertaining to (13)

ʒe-lang *aj.* at hand, belonging to, dependent on (13)

langaþ (langaðas) *m.* longing (14)

lange (lenǵ, lenǵest) *av.* long, a long time (286)

langian *II* long for, yearn, be grieved (14)

langian *II* send for, summon (6)

langung (~a) *f.* longing (14)

lann (~a) *f.* fetter, chains (2)

lár (~a) *f.* instruction, teaching, counsel (198)

láréow (~as) *m.* teacher (18)

lást (~as) *m.* track, trail (72)

~weard (~as) *m.* heir; persecutor (257)

~word *n.sg.* fame after death (631)

lata (~n) *m.* laggard (28)

latian *II* delay (28)

láttéow (~as) *m.* leader (12)

latu (lata) *f.* delay (28)

láþ (~) *n.* foe, harm, evil, enmity: *aj.* loathly, hostile (197)

~wende *aj.* hateful, hostile (213)

láþ *see* líðan

léac *see* lúcan

léad *n.sg.* lead (metal) (5)

léaf (~a) *f.* permission, leave (43)

léaf (~) *n.* leaf (of a plant) (43)

ȝe-léafa (~n) *m.* belief, faith (79)

léafnes-word *n.sg.* permission (631)

léag *see* léogan

leahtor (leahtras) *m.* vice, sin, evil (57)

léan (~) *n.* reward; retribution (151)

léan [<*leahan<*lahan] (lóg, 6, læȝen) *6* blame, vilify: be~ blame; dissuade from (57)

léanian *II* reward, requite, pay (151)

léap *m.sg.* torso, trunk (1)

léas (~) *n.* falsehood (224)

léas *aj.* loose, free, false, lacking: *suff.* lacking, without (224)

~líć *aj.* false (322)

léas *see* léosan

-léast *suff.* lacking, without (224)

léasung (~a) *f.* deceit, falsehood (224)

léat *see* lútan

leax *m.sg.* salmon (2)

leććan (leahte) *I* water, sprinkle; flow over (3)

lecgan (leȝde) *I* lay: lástas ~ go, journey: á~ lay down; lay aside, give up; impose; diminish; withhold: be~ belay, lay upon: of~ lay down (160)

leðer (~u) *n.* leather (6)

léf *aj.* weak, infirm (3)

leȝen *see* licgan

leȝer (~u) *n.* couch, resting place, lying, lair (160)

ȝe-leȝere *n.sg.* cohabitation (160)

lemman *I* hinder, oppress, trouble (6)

lendan *I* come ashore, land (231)

leń *see* lange

lenȝan *I* lengthen, delay (286)

lenȝe *aj.* pertaining to, belonging to; related; at hand (286)

lenȝra, lenȝest *see* lang

lengten *m.sg.* spring-time (9)

lenȝu *f.sg.* length (286)

léo (~n) *m.f.* lion, lioness (7)

léod *m.sg.* (free?) man; prince (277)

léod (~e) *f.* nation; people (277)

~hata (~n) *m.* tyrant (75)

~hwæt *aj.* courageous (47)

léodan (éa, u, o) *2* grow (9)

léoðian *II* sing; sound (28)

léof *aj.* beloved, dear, friendly (426)

~tǽl(e) *aj.* kind, loving; agreeable (30)

~wende *aj.* amiable, pleasing (213)

léofian *II* be dear (426)

léogan (léag, lugon, o) *2* falsify, lie, belie: ȝe~ deceive (52)

léoht *n.sg.* light; daylight; world (279)

léoht *aj.* light, not heavy; agile, swift; light, bright, clear: ~e *av.* brightly, clearly; gladly (279)

~fæt (-fatu) *n.* light-vessel, candelabrum, luminary (sun or moon) (31)

léohtian *II* be light, shine (279)

leolc *see* lácan

léoma (~n) *m.* gleam, light, splendor (49)

leort *see* lǽtan

léosan (léas, luron, o) *2* lose: be~ lose; deprive: for~ lose, lack; destroy (224)

léoþ (~) *n.* song, poem, lay (28)

leppan *I* feed (1)

lesan (æ, ǽ, e) *5* collect, gather: á~ select, pick out (6) lét *see* lǽtan

lettan *I* slow up, hinder, prevent; withstand (28)

libban (lifde) *III* be, live: be~ deprive of life (600)

líċ (~) *n.* form, body, corpse (322)

~fæt *n.sg.* body (31)

~hama (~n) *m.* body (93)

-líċ *aj.suff.* form or quality (*of first element of compound*) (322)

ȝe-líċ (~) *n.* similarity: *aj.* like, similar, equal to; likely (322)

~ness (~a) *f.* likeness, image (322)

líca (~n) *m.* image, statue (322)

liccian *II* lick (1)

ȝe-líċe *av.* likewise, also, as (322)

-líċe *av.suff.* in manner like (*first element of compound*) (322)

líċettan *I* make like, simulate (322)

licgan (læȝ, lágon, leȝen) *I-5* lie, be situated; lie down, lie dead; fail: á~ fail, cease: be~ lie around, encompass: for~ fornicate: ȝe~ lie, be situated; lie along, extend; cease (160)

líċian *II* please, gratify, like (15)

líċiend-líċ *aj.* agreeable, pleasant (322)

ȝe-líċum *av.dat.* likewise (322)

líc-wierðe *aj.* pleasing, acceptable (227)

lid (~u) *n.* sailing vessel, ship (62)

lida (~n) *m.* sailor (62)

lidon *see* líðan

Líða *m.sg.* June and July (1)

líðan (láþ, lidon, i) *1* go, leave, part from; journey, sail: be~ separate from, be bereft of, deprive of: ȝe~ depart; complete a journey (62)

líðe *aj.av.* gentle, gracious, friendly; gently, kindly (68)

líðend (~e) *ppl.m.* traveler, sailor (62)

liðere *f.sg.* leather sling (6)

liðian *II* lead (62)

liðian *II* unloose; escape: á~ detach: be~ dismember (48)

on-líðian *II* become tractable, yield (68)

líðs *see* liss

liðu (liða) *f.* ship (?); retinue (?) (62)

liðu-, lioðu- *pref.* pertaining to the hands (skills) or body (48)

~cræft (~as) *m.* skill (223)

~cǽȝe *f.sg.* fleshly key (4)

~fæst *aj.* skillful (372)

~líċ *aj.* bodily (322)

~rún *f.sg.* wise counsel (?) (78)

~wác *aj.* with supple limbs (30)

líeðre *aj.av.* bad(ly) (3)

líefan *I* allow, permit: á~ allow, grant; hand over, yield up: ȝe~ allow, grant (43)

ȝe-líefan *I* believe, hope, trust (79)

ȝe-líefan *I* to make dear (426)

líeȝ (líeȝas) *m.* fire, flame (136)

~spiwol *aj.* fire-vomiting (12)

líeȝen *aj.* flaming, flashing (136)

líeȝet (~ta, ~tu) *f.n.* flash of lightning (136)

líeȝnan *I* give the lie to, deny (52)

líehtan *I* illumine: ȝeond~, on~ enlighten (279)

líehting (~a) *f.* illumination (279)

líesan *I* release, redeem (224)

-líest *suff.* lacking, without (224)

líexan *I* shine, gleam (279)

líf (~) *n.* life (600)

~bisiȝ *aj.* struggling for life (39)

~fæst *aj.* vigorous (372)

~ȝe-twinnan *m.pl.* twins (3)

~wela (~n) *m.* (worldly or heavenly) riches (266)

be-lífan (á, i, i) *1* remain (78)

lifen (~a) *f.* food (600)

lifer (~a) *f.* liver (organ) (78)

lifian *II* be, live (600)

-lifiende *ppl.suff.* alive (600)

lílie (lílian) *f.* lily (1)

lim (~u) *n.* limb, member; branch (30)

~wæstm (~as) *m.* growth, stature (96)

lím *m.sg.* lime, mortar (2)

ȝe-limp (~u) *n.* occurrence; accident (45)

limpan (a, u, u) *3* happen, come to pass (45)

lind (~a) *f.* linden-tree, linden-wood shield (33)

~croda (~n) *m.* collision of shields, shield-attack (5)

linden *aj.* of linden wood (33)

líne (línan) *f.* rope; line, row; canon, rule (4)

linnan (a, u, u) *3* part from, lose: á~ set free (11)

lin-sǽd *n.sg.* linseed (1)

lioðu- *see* liðu

líon [<*líohan<*líhan] (láh, *def.*) *1* lend, give, grant (58)

líoran (líorde/líorode, ʒe-loren) *I-II-2* go, depart; die: ofer~ transgress; prevaricate (7)

liornere (liorneras) *m.* learner, pupil; scholar (18)

liornian *II* learn; plan, devise (18)

liornung *f.sg.* learning (18)

liss/líðs (~a) *f.* favor, grace, peace; joy (68)

lissan *I* subdue (68)

list (~as) *m.* cunning, guile, artifice (24)

~hendiʒ *aj.* skillful (310)

listum *av.dat.* skillfully, cunningly (24)

liþ (liðu) *n.* limb, member (48)

líþ (~) *n.* strong cider (1)

~wǽʒe *n.sg.* beaker of strong cider (9)

loc/locen (~u) *n.* lock, bolt; prison (117)

loca (~n) *m.* lock, bolt; imprisonment, prison, stronghold; any container or enclosure (117)

locc (~as) *m.* lock of hair (9)

locen *see* loc, lúcan

lócian *II* look, see, observe (31)

loden *see* léodan

loða (~n) *m.* mantel, cloak (1)

lof *m.n.sg.* praise, glory (125)

~sum *aj.* praiseworthy (125)

lof *m.sg.* help, guidance; protection (5)

lofian *II* praise (125)

lóg *see* féa-lóg, léan

loga (~n) *m.* liar, traitor (52)

logen *see* léogan

ʒe-lóme *av.* often (25)

-lora *m.suff.* loser (224)

loren *see* léosan, líoran

losian *II* lose one's way; escape (224)

lot (~u) *n.* guile, deceit (3)

lúcan (éa, u, o) *2* close, lock; intertwine, link, weave; set (a jewel): be~ close, shut; preserve from: ʒe~ weave: on~ unlock, open, disclose (117)

lúcan (éa, u, o) *2* pull up, pluck: to~ pull to pieces, destroy (3)

ludon *see* léodan

lufen (~a) *f.* comfort (?); hope (?); love, beloved object (?) (2)

lufian *II* love (426)

luf-sum *aj.* loving; lovable (426)

lufu (lufa; lufan) *f.* love; beloved object (426)

lugon *see* léogan

lumpon *see* limpan

lungor *aj.* swift (47)

lungre *av.* quickly, at once, suddenly (47)

luron *see* léosan

lust (~as) *m.* joy, pleasure; desire; lust (118)

lustum *av.dat.* gladly (118)

lútan (éa, u, o) *2* bow down (4)

ʒe-lútian *II* lie hid, lurk (4)

lybb *n.sg.* drug, poison; magic (1)

~lác (~) *f.n.* witchcraft (200)

lyft (~a) *m.f.n.* air, sky (94)

~fæt *n.sg.* vessel of the sky, moon (31)

lyʒe *m.sg.* lie, falsehood (52)

~torn *n.sg.* feigned grievance (45)

lyʒen (~a) *f.* falsehood (52)

lynd *f.sg.* fat (4)

lyre (~as) *m.* loss, harm (224)

lystan *I* desire; cause desire: ʒe-, of-lysted *ppl.aj.* desirous (118)

lysu *aj.* false, bad (2)

lýt *indecl.sb.aj.* small amount, little: *av.* very little, not at all (123)

~hwón *n.sg.* few: *av.* very little, not at all (123)

lýt/lýtle (lǽs, lǽst) *av.* little (less, least) (123)

lýtel (lǽssa, lǽst) *aj.* small, little (123)

lýtes-ná *av.* almost, nearly, within a little (123)

lytiȝian *II* become guileful (3)

lýtlian *II* grow less, lessen: ȝe~ belittle (123)

lǽćan *I* spring up (200)

lǽććan *I* seize, capture (2)

lǽće (lǽćas) *m.* doctor, physician (15)

lǽdan *I* lead, bring: á~ lead, lead out, bring out, produce: for~ mislead, lead to disaster: ȝe~ lead, bring; go: on~ bring: oþ~ lead away, withdraw: wiþ~ rescue (240)

Lǽden *aj.* Latin (1)

lǽdend (~as) *m.* one who excuses (3)

lǽfan *I* leave, bequeath (78)

lǽȝ *see* licgan

lǽȝen *see* léan

lǽl (~a) *f.* rod, strap; bruise, wound (3)

lǽla (~n) *m.* bruise, wound (3)

lǽlian *II* be bruised (3)

lǽmen *aj.* loamy, earthen (13)

lǽn *f.n.sg.* loan, (transitory) gift: *pref.* transitory (58)

lǽnan *I* lend, grant (58)

lǽne *aj.* on loan, temporary, transitory, unstable (58)

lǽran *I* teach, instruct, persuade (198)

lǽrend (~) *m.* teacher (198)

lǽr-ȝe-dœfe *aj.* fitting, proper to be learned (36)

lǽriȝ (~) *m.* border, edge (3)

lǽs *see* lesan

lǽs, lǽssa, lǽst *see* lýt, lýtel

lǽst (~a) *f.* completion (?) (72)

lǽstan *I* carry out, execute; follow, serve, stand by, back (someone): ȝe~ serve, perform; last, endure: full~ help, protect (72)

lǽt *aj.* late, slow, sluggish (28)

lǽtan (lét/leort, é, ǽ) *7* let, allow, cause (someone to do something): á~ let, allow; leave, give up; release, forgive; relinquish, lose, abandon, neglect: for~ allow, permit; leave, let go, release, forgive; surrender, lose, abandon; reject, renounce; abstain from, avoid: of~ leave, relinquish: on~ let go, loosen (283)

lǽte (*comp.* lator) *av.* late, slowly, at length (28)

lǽw-finger (-fingras) *m.* forefinger; accusing finger (?) (1)

lǽþþu *f.sg.* offence, harm; sorrow (197)

M

má *indecl.n.sg.* more (of) (626)

má *av.* more, furthermore (626)

má *see* mićle

macian *II* make (16)

maðelian *II* speak, discourse, make a speech (95)

máðum (máðmas) *m.* treasure, jewel, ornament (65)

~siȝel *n.sg.* brilliant and precious jewel (11)

mág *aj.* bad, importunate (3)

maga *m.sg.* maw, belly (1)

mága (~n) *m.* son, relative, descendant; man (207)

magan (mæȝ, meaht/miht, meahte/mihte) *prp.* can, be able, have power to; have power against, avail (1596)

máge *see* mǽȝe

mágister (mágistras) *m.* teacher, master (2)

magu (mæcgas) *m.* kinsman, son, man (102)

~timber *n.sg.* child, son; progeny (39)

malscrung (~a) *f.* magical charm (1)

mámrian *II* think out, plan (1)

man *impers.pron.* one, they (1030)

man *see* munan

mán (~) *n.* crime, guilt, wickedness: *aj.* wicked, false, base (123)

~for-dǽdla (~n) *m.* evil-doer (530)

~for-wyrht (~) *n.* sin (538)

~slagu *f.sg.* cruel blow (97)

~swara (~n) *m.* perjurer (96)

~weorc (~) *n.* sin: *aj.* sinful (538)

ȝe-mána (~n) *m.* community, dealings, intercourse (29)

mang (?) *n.sg.* company, commerce, intercourse (?) (51)

ȝe-mang (~) *n.* mingling; assembly, group (51)

manian *II* exhort, urge (12)

maniȝ *aj.* many a: *pl.* many (275)

~feald *aj.* manifold, various (27)

~fealdian *II* multiply (27)

mann (menn) *m.* man, human being; name of M-rune (1030)

~þwǽre *aj.* gentle, kind (8)

~þwǽr-ness *f.sg.* gentleness, kindness (8)

manna (~n) *m.* man, human being (1030)

manna *n.sg.* manna (1)

mára *see* miċel

marma (~n) *m.* marble (2)

martir (~as) *m.* martyr (7)

á-masian *II* amaze (1)

máwan (éo, éo, á) *7* mow; cut down (3)

máþ *see* míðan

méagol *aj.* impressive, mighty (5)

meaht/miht (~a) *f.* might, power: *aj.* mighty (1596)

~iȝ *aj.* mighty, powerful (1596)

meaht *see* magan

mealt *see* meltan

mearc *f.n.sg.* mark, measurement, boundary; district: ȝe~ what is designated (73)

mearcian *II* mark, stain; designate; design; set a limit, measure (73)

mearg *m.sg.* marrow (1)

~cofa (~n) *m.* bone (27)

mearh (méaras) *m.* steed (29)

mearn *see* murnan

mearu *aj.* tender, soft (1)

méċe (méċas) *m.* sword (27)

méd (~a) *f.* meed, reward (10)

med- *pref.* middling-; un- (192)

~spǿdiȝ *aj.* unprosperous (137)

~trym-ness (~a) *f.* infirmity, sickness (82)

~wís *aj.* dull, stupid (764)

medeme *aj.* small, middling (192)

ȝe-medemian *II* moderate; humiliate (192)

medu *m.sg.* mead (68)

~rǽden *f.sg.* responsibility for serving mead (174)

~scierwen *f.sg.* terror, despair; serving of (fateful, deadly) drink (?); deprivation of mead, of prosperity, of revelry (?) (52)

meld (~a) *f.* proclamation (18)

melda (~n) *m.* reporter, informer (18)

meldan *I* proclaim: to~ scandalize (18)

meldian *II* proclaim, announce (18)

mele-déaw *m.sg.* honey-dew, nectar (16)

meltan (ea, u, o) *3* disintegrate, dissolve, melt (17)

mene (menas) *m.* necklace (2)

menȝan *I* mingle, mix, disturb; combine, compound (51)

meniȝu *f.sg.* company, host, multitude (275)

mennen (~) *n.* maid, slave girl (1030)

mennisc *n.pl.* people: *aj.* human (1030)

meord (~a) f. reward (6)

méorring (~a) *f.* obstacle, hindrance (?) (1)

meotod *m.sg.* fate, Creator, God (249)

meotu (?) (~) *f.* thought, meditation (?) (146)

méowle (méowlan) *f.* young woman, lady (11)

meox *n.sg.* dirt, dung (1)

mere (~) *m.* pond, lake, sea (84)

merȝen *see* morgen

merian *I* purify (11)

mersc (~as) *m.* marsh, swamp (84)

ȝe-met (~u) *n.* measure, limit, portion; rule, law; faculty, power: *aj.* fitting, proper (146) metan (æ, ǽ, e) 5 measure, mete out, measure off or cover (a distance) (146)

mete (mettas) m. food (26)

metend m.sg. measurer, God (146)

metgian II meditate; mediate, moderate (146)

metgung (~a) f. moderation, mediation (146)

metian II consider, ponder, attend to (146)

miċél (mára, mǽst) aj. large, big, great (626)

miċele (má, mǽst) av. much (more, most) (626)

miċelian II become big, make big, increase (626)

miċelum av. greatly, much (626)

mid av.prep. at the same time, together, likewise; with, in the company of, by means of (1134)

~wist m.f.sg. presence (4189)

midd aj. middle, the middle of (192)

middan-ȝeard m.sg. world, earth (167)

midde f.sg. middle (192)

middel m.sg. middle (part), center (192)

mídl (~) n. bit (of a bridle) (2)

midon see míðan

míðan (máþ, midon, i) 1 avoid, conceal, dissimulate (17)

mierċe m.pl. men of the borders, marches (73)

mierċe n.sg. darkness, evil: aj.av. dark(ly), evil(ly) (9)

ȝe-mierċe (-mierċu) f. boundary (73)

mierċed aj. darkened (?); designated (?) (9; 73)

mierċels m.f.sg. mark, aim; tonsure (73)

mierðu f.sg. affliction, disturbance (?) (11)

mierran I harm, damage, mar; disturb, obstruct (11)

mierrelse f.sg. hindrance, stumbling-block (11)

miht see meaht

míl (~a) f. mile (6)

~pæþ (-paðas) m. road measured in miles (17)

milde aj.av. gentle, generous, merciful; graciously, mercifully (242)

milds (~a) f. kindness, mercy; joy (242)

mildsian II be merciful, pity; make merciful, soften (242)

mildsung (~a) f. mercy (242)

min-dóm (~as) m. state of exile (?); faintheartedness (?) (5)

minne aj. harmful, evil (5)

minsian II lessen, diminish (5)

mioluc f.sg. milk (2)

mis- pref. different, various; bad, wrong, perverse (21)

~ȝe-dwield n.sg. evil deceit (33)

~líċ, ~e aj.av. various(ly) (29)

~miċel aj. of small quantity, few (?) (626)

missan I miss (29)

missere (misseru) n. half-year, (summer or winter) season (8)

mist (~as) m. mist (15)

~iȝ aj. misty (15)

mitta (~n) m. (wet or dry) measure (of about a bushel) (9)

mittan I meet, meet with, find (9)

mitting f.sg. conflict, clash (9)

mód (~) n. mind, heart, soul, spirit, disposition; courage; pride; arrogance; greatness, magnificence: suff. -minded (840)

~héap (~as) m. bold troop (56)

~iȝ aj. noble-minded, high-spirited; courageous, bold; hearty, earnest; proud, arrogant, willful (840)

~þrýþ f.sg. violence of character (33)

módgian II behave proudly; rage (840)

módor (dat.sg. mœ́der) f.sg. mother (60)

molde (moldan) f. dust, earth (as material) (46)

molsnian II molder; wilt (2)

molten see meltan

móna m.sg. moon (30)

mónaþ (~) m. month (30)

mór (~as) *m.* fen; upland (16)

~heald *aj.* on the hillside (?); in the moors (?) (26)

morðor (~) *n.* slaying, murder; torment, torture; deadly sin (54)

morgen/merȝen (morgnas) *m.* morning, morrow, next day (50)

mornen *see* murnan

morþ *n.sg.* death; slaying, murder; deadly sin (54)

mós (~) *n.* food (10)

ȝe-mót (~) *n.* meeting, assembly, meeting-place; encounter (78)

mótan (mót, móst, móste) *prp.* be permitted to, may (298)

moþþe (moþþan) *f.* moth (1)

mucg-wyrt (~a) *f.* mugwort, *Artemisia vulgaris* (1)

múða (~n) *m.* mouth, opening, entrance (75)

multon *see* meltan

munan (man, manst, munde) *prp.* bear in mind, consider, recall, remember: on~ think worthy of; consider fit for (419)

mund (~a) *f.* hand; protection, trust (28)

~byrd *f.sg.* protection (652)

~háls *f.sg.* protection (?) (272)

ȝe-mund-byrdan *I* protect (652)

mundian *II* protect (28)

munt (~as) *m.* mountain (21)

munuc (~as) *m.* monk (3)

múr (~as) *m.* wall (1)

murc *aj.* wretched (2)

murcnian *II* complain, grieve (2)

murnan (ea, murnon/murndon, o) *3* care about, mourn for, regret (39)

must *m.sg.* new wine, must (1)

be-mútian *II* exchange for (1)

múþ (múðas) *m.* mouth, opening, entrance (75)

mylen-scearp *aj.* sharp from the grindstone (?) (1)

-mynd *suff.* mind, of the mind; minded, mindful (419)

ȝe-mynd (~) *f.n.* memory, mind, thought, feeling (419)

~iȝ *aj.* mindful (419)

ȝe-mynde *aj.* mindful (419)

myndiȝian *II* call to mind, recall; admonish (419)

myne (~) *m.* remembrance, thought; regard for, love; desire (419)

mynian *II* intend, be implied; remember (419)

mynle (mynla) *f.* desire (419)

mynster (~u) *m.* monastery (2)

myntan *I* intend, think, resolve (419)

myrðe *aj.* murderous (54)

myrðra (~n) *m.* murderer (54)

á-myrȝan *I* be merry (8)

myrȝe(n) *aj.* joyous, merry (8)

myrȝþ (~a) *f.* merriment, joy (8)

mysci *n.pl.(Lat.)* flies (1)

ȝe-mæć *aj.* suitable, companionable (16)

ȝe-mæćća (~n) *m.* companion; spouse (16)

mæcg(a) (~as; ~a) *m.* kinsman; son; man (102)

mæðel (~u) *n.* council, meeting; speech; contest, battle (95)

~híeȝende *ppl.aj.* deliberating (12)

mæðlan *I* discourse, make a speech (95)

mǽȝ (mágas) *m.* kinsman, relation (207)

~burg *f.sg.* group of kinsmen, clan (398)

~wlite (-wlitas) *m.* aspect, form, image, species (218)

mæȝden (~u) *n.* maid, young woman (54)

mǽȝ(e)/máge *f.sg.* kinswoman (207)

mǽȝe *aj.* related (207)

mæȝen (~) *n.* might, power, "main"; force, multitude, army: *pref.* mighty; very (1596)

~ágende *ppl.aj.* powerful (370)

mæȝenian *II* gain strength (1596)

mæȝ(eþ) (~) *f.* maiden, unmarried woman (54)

mǽȝþ (mǽȝða) *f.* clan, tribe, nation (207)

mǽʒþa *m.sg.* mayweed, *Anthemis cotula, A. nobilis* (54)

mǽl (~a) *f.* speech; contest (95)

mǽl (~) *n.* time, point of time, season; meal-time, meal; mark, sign, token; decoration; sword (57)

ʒe-mǽl *aj.* variegated (57)

mǽlan *I* discourse, speak (95)

ʒe-mǽlan *I* mark, stain; adorn (57)

mǽle(d) *aj.* marked, stained; adorned (57)

mǽnan *I* complain, lament; observe, mention, mean (23)

mǽne *aj.* wicked (123)

ʒe-mǽne *aj.* common, mutual, general, shared (29)

ʒe-mǽn-ness *f.sg.* fellowship (29)

ʒe-mǽn-scipe *m.sg.* fellowship (340)

-mǽr *aj.suff.* illustrious, noble (283)

mǽran *I* declare, make known; glorify (283)

ʒe-mǽran *I* establish, fix limits (12)

mǽrðu (mǽrða) *f.* fame, glory (283)

mǽre *aj.* illustrious, noble, splendid (283)

ʒe-mǽre (-mǽru) *n.* boundary: *pl.* district (12)

mǽrsian *II* extol (283)

mæsse (mæssan) *f.* mass (religious service) (6)

mæssere (mæsseras) *m.* (mass-)priest (6)

mæst (~as) *m.* mast (of a ship) (6)

mæst *f.sg.* mast, food for swine (6)

mǽst *n.sg.* most (of), very much, most (626)

mǽst *see* miċel, *aj.*, miċle, *av.*

á-mæstan *I* feed on mast (6)

mæt *see* metan

ʒe-mǽtan *I* dream (4)

mǽte *aj.* moderate, slight, small (146)

ʒe-mǽte *av.* fitly, properly (146)

mǽting *f.sg.* dream (4)

mǽw (~as) *m.* mew, sea-gull (3)

mǽþ *f.sg.* measure, fitness; what is meet, right (1)

mœ́dan *I* take on oneself (840)

-mœ́de *aj.suff.* -minded (840)

ʒe-mœ́de *n.* consent, approval: *aj.* agreeable, pleasing (840)

mœ́dla *m.sg.* pride (840)

mœ́dren *aj.* maternal, on the mother's side (60)

-mœ́du *f.suff.* mind, spirit (840)

mœ́ðe *aj.* tired, weary (18)

mœ́ðgian *II* tire out (18)

mœ́san *I* eat (10)

mœ́tan *I* meet, meet with, find (78)

ʒe-mœ́ting (~a) *f.* meeting, encounter (78)

-mœ́ttu (-mœ́tta) *f.suff.* pride (840)

N

ná *av.* not, never, not at all (377)

~hwæðer *pron.* neither (of two) (186)

~hwǽr *av.* nowhere, not at all (136)

nabban (næfde) *III* not have, lack (771)

naca (~n) *m.* ship, vessel (12)

nacod *aj.* naked, bare, sleek (12)

n'ágan (n'áh, n'áhst, n'áhte) *prp.* not have, lack (370)

náht/ná-wiht *n.sg.* nothing, naught: *av.* not (25)

nam, námon *see* niman

nama (~n) *m.* name (233)

ʒe-namian *II* name, mention (233)

ʒe-namn *aj.* of the same name (233)

nán *pron.aj.* none, no one, no (850)

náp *see* nípan

nard *m.sg.* nard, ointment (1)

nást, nát *see* nytan

nát-hwelċ *indef.pron.* (I) do not know which, someone or other (477)

nát-hwǽr *av.* (I) do not know where, somewhere or other (136)

nát-hwæt *indef.pron.* (I) do not know what, something or other (521)

náwðer *pron.* neither (of two) (186)

nĕ *av.cj.* not, no; neither, nor (1782)

né *see* néo

néad *see* níed "need"

neah *av.* enough (107)

-neah *see* -nugan

néah (néarra, níehst) *aj.* near; late (120)

néah (néar, níehst) *av.* near(ly); lately (120)

néah *prep.* near to (120)

~wist *m.f.sg.* neighborhood, vicinity (4189)

ȝe-neahh(iȝ)e *av.* enough, very much; often; instantly; earnestly (107)

ȝe-néahsen *aj.* near, close together (120)

neaht *see* niht

nealles *av.* not at all, by no means (1600)

néa-lǽćan *I* approach, draw near to (200)

néan *av.* from near at hand, near (120)

nearu (nearwa) *f.n.* difficulty, distress: *aj.* narrow, confined, restricted (62)

~cræft (~as) *m.* protective cunning (223)

nearwe *av.* closely, restrictedly (62)

nearwian *II* confine, oppress, press hard (62)

néat (~) *n.* livestock, cattle (24)

néat *see* néotan

ȝe-néat (~as) *m.* comrade, follower, retainer (11)

nebb (~) *n.* face; bill (of a bird); beak-shaped object; boss (12)

nefa (~n) *m.* nephew; grandson (5)

nefne/nymðe *cj.prep.* except, unless (63)

nemnan (nemde, nemned) *I* call by name, declare, proclaim (233)

né(o) (néäs) *m.* corpse (4)

~bedd *n.sg.* death-bed; bed of spirits (hell) (33)

~fugol (-fuglas) *m.* carrion bird (96)

néod/níed (~a) *f.* wish, desire, pleasure (83)

néomian *II* ring out, sound (2)

ȝe-néopan (éa, u, o) *2* oppress; surprise, come upon (?) (1)

Neorxna-wang *m.sg.* Paradise (76)

néosian *II* visit, frequent; attack (36)

néotan (éa, u, o) *2* use, enjoy: be~

take away (26)

nepp (?) *aj.*(?) deprived of, lacking (?) (1)

ner (~) *n.* refuge, safety (145)

nerian *I* save, deliver; defend (145)

Neriend *m.sg.* the Saviour (145)

neru *f.sg.* refuge, salvation; food (145)

nesan (æ, ǽ, e) *5* survive (145)

-ness (~a) *f.suff.* state or condition (*of first element of compound*)

nest *n.sg.* food, provisions (145)

nest *n.sg.* nest (12)

nett (~) *n.* net (35)

nicor (~as) *m.* water-monster (5)

niðan(e) *av.* from below, below (64)

niðemest *av.* deepest (64)

niðer *av.* down, below (64)

~heald *aj.* inclined, turned downward (16)

~weard *aj.* inclined, turned downward (882)

ȝe-niðerian *II* abuse, humiliate (64)

ȝe-níðla (~n) *m.* enemy; enmity (148)

níed/néad (~a) *f.* need, necessity; distress, trouble; force, violence; *pl.* fetters; name of N-rune (70)

~bád *f.sg.* forced contribution, toll (15)

~laðu *f.sg.* pressing summons (11)

níed *see* néod "wish"

níedan *I* compel, force, urge (70)

níehst *see* á-níehst, néah

ȝe-nierwan *I* confine (62)

níeten (~) *n.* small livestock (24)

níewan *av.* newly, lately (78)

níewe *aj.av.* new(ly) (78)

níewian *II* begin (as something new), happen (for the first time) (78)

níewunga *av.* anew (78)

nifol *aj.* dark (2)

nigoða *aj.* ninth (24)

nigun *num.* nine (24)

~tíene *num.* nineteen (24)

niht/neaht (~) *f.* night, darkness; *pl* (astronomical, 24-hour) days (214)

niman (a, á, u) *4* take, receive, get

seize: á~ take away (from): be~ deprive of, rob: for~ take away, destroy: ʒe~ take; assume, receive; bring, carry; seize, carry off: æt~ take away (from) (180)

níosan *I* visit, frequent; attack (36)

niowol *aj.* precipitous, steep; headlong; obscure, deep (19)

ʒe-nip (~u) *n.* darkness (18)

nípan (á, i, i) *1* grow dark (18)

nistlian *II* build a nest (12)

niþ *n.sg.* abyss (?) (64)

níþ (níðas) *m.* force, enmity, strife; battle, war; affliction, grief (148)

niþþas *m.pl.* men (30)

ʒe-nóg *aj.* sufficient, plenty of (107)

-nohte *see* -nugan

nolde *see* nyllan

nón *f.sg.* ninth canonical hour (3 P.M.) (1)

norðan *av.* from the north (36)

norðerne *aj.* northern (36)

norþ *aj.av.* north, northern, northward (36)

~mest *aj.* northmost (36)

nóse (nósan) *f.* promontory (24)

nosu (nosa) *f.* nose (24)

nót (~as) *m.* mark, letter (1)

noten *see* néotan

nóþ *f.sg.* daring: -nóþ *suff.* (*in pers. names*): nóðe *av.dat.* boldly (37)

nú *av.cj.* now, now that (676)

~þá *av.* now (*emphatic*); just now (1692)

nugan (neah, nohte) *prp.* suffice: be~ need, require, enjoy: ʒe~ suffice, not be wanting (107)

numen *see* niman

nuton *see* néotan

ʒe-nyht *f.n.sg.* sufficiency (107)

~sum *aj.* abundant; contented (137)

nyllan (nylle, nylt, nolde) *anv.* not wish, be unwilling (998)

nymðe *see* nefne

nytan (nát, nást, nysse/nyste) *prp.* not to know (764)

nytt *f.sg.* advantage, use; duty, office:

aj. useful (26)

nyttian *II* use, enjoy (26)

nyttung (~a) *f.* profit, advancement (26)

nǽdl (~a) *f.* needle (2)

nǽdre (nǽdran) *f.* snake, serpent (13)

nǽfre *av.* never (296)

nǽʒan *I* draw near to, address; accost, assail (20)

næʒl (~as) *m.* nail, stud (22)

næʒled *aj.* nailed, studded (22)

be-nǽman *I* deprive of (180)

nǽniʒ *aj.pron.* none, no one, no (850)

nǽre, nǽron *see* wesan

nærende (?) *m.pl.*(?) deliverers, saviors (?) (145)

næs *see* nesan, wesan

næss (~as) *m.* headland, ness; cliff; abyss, pit (24)

næsse *f.sg.* headland, promontory (24)

ʒe-nǽstan *I* struggle (1)

nǽtan *I* afflict, oppress (1)

nœ́ðan *I* dare, risk, try, venture on (37)

nœ́ðing *f.sg.* daring, audacity (37)

O

óc *see* acan

óðer *aj.* second, other (269)

of *prep.* from, out of: *av.* off, away (654)

~dúne *av.* down, downward (25)

~dæle (~) *n.* descent; abyss (10)

~hende *aj.* absent, lost (310)

of- *vb.pref.* (*perfective & intensive*) (83)

ofen (~as) *m.* furnace, oven (15)

ofer *prep.av.* over, above, on, upon, among, throughout; over, across, beyond; towards, contrary to, in spite of, against; above, move than; after; without (622)

ofer- *pref.* (*with sbs. & ajs.*) over, above; very, very great, superior, excessive (ly); (*with vbs. & avs.*) over, above, beyond (622)

~bæc *av.* backward(s) (13)

~ʒeatu *f.sg.* oblivion (166)

~ʒietel *aj.* forgetful (166)

~ʒiet-ness *f.sg.* forgetfulness (166)

~hléoðor *aj.* inattentive, unhearing (62)

~holt (~) *n.* shield (?); spear (?) (32)

~hyʒd (~u) *n.* pride; arrogance (571)

~hylmend (~) *n.* prevaricator (164)

~mód *n.sg.* overconfidence: *aj.* proud, insolent (840)

~mæcga *m.sg.* distinguished man (102)

~mǽde (~) *n.* pride (840)

~pynde (?) *aj.* overflowing (?); over-repressed (?) (2)

ófer (ófras) *m.* river-bank (7)

ofett *n.sg.* fruit (11)

offrian *II* offer sacrifice (to God) (1)

ofost (~a) *f.* haste (56)

ofstum *av.* hastily (56)

oft *av.* often (273)

óga (~n) *m.* fear, horror (218)

óht *f.sg.* persecution, terror (22)

ól *see* alan

ó-leććan (-lecte; -lehte) *I* please, appease (4)

óm *m.sg.* rust (3)

~iʒ *aj.* rusty (3)

on *av.* on, from (4747)

on/in *prep.* in, on, into, upon; at, to, towards, among; during; in respect of (4747)

on-, an-, *pref.* against, opposite, parallel to, towards, in reply to (*weakened forms of* and-, *denoting inception, perfection, antithesis, intensification, reversive action, separation*) (294)

on-bid *n.sg.* expectation, waiting (150)

on-bǽru *f.sg.* self-restraint (652)

on-drysne *aj.* terrible (3)

ónettan *I* hasten, hasten on (18)

on-foran *av.prep.* to the fore, forward, in front of, before (223)

on-ʒeador *av.* together (86)

on-ʒeʒn *av.prep.* opposite, against, over against, with; towards, in reply (29)

on-hindan *av.* behind (30)

on-hóhsnian (?) *II* restrain, put a stop to; hamstring (?) (3)

on-hǽle *aj.* secret, concealed (164)

on-lást(e) *prep.* behind, in pursuit of (72)

on-mǿtan *I* paint, cover (1)

on-níed (~a) *f.* compulsion (?); oppression (?) (70)

on-riht *aj.* true, proper, right; partaking of (?) (417)

on-scuniend-líć *aj.* to be shunned, abominable (2)

on-síen *f.sg.* lack, want (5)

on-síen (~a) *f.* face, form, aspect, sight (494)

on-síene *aj.* visible (494)

on-sǽʒe *aj.* impending (27)

on-wealg *aj.* intact, whole (2)

on-weʒ *av.* away (209)

on-wended-ness (~a) *f.* change (213)

on-wille *aj.* agreeable (998)

on-wist *f.sg.* habitation (4189)

on-æðele *aj.* natural to (397)

on-ǿʒan *I* fear (218)

open *aj.* open, evident, clear (32)

openian *II* open, manifest, reveal (32)

or- *pref.* (*intensive & privative*) (89)

ór (~) *n.* beginning, origin; front (14)

óra (~n) *m.* bank, border (1)

orc (~as) *m.* cup (3)

orc-néas *m.pl.* evil spirits of the dead (1)

or-cnǽwe *aj.* well-known, evident (63)

ord (~) *n.* point, spear; beginning, source; front rank, best of a class; chief, prince (83)

óret *m.sg.* battle, strife; labor (16)

óretta (~n) *m.* warrior (16)

ʒe-órettan *I* disgrace, confound (16)

orf (~) *n.* cattle (1)

or-fierme *aj.* poor in, lacking; useless (30)

organ (~as) *m.* canticle, chant (4)

organan *f.pl.* musical instrument (4)

or-ʒiete *aj.* manifest (9)

or-hlytte *aj.* without a share in, destitute (20)

or-ieldu *f.sg.* great age (179)

or-leȝ- *pref.* hostile, of war (24)

~ćéap *m.sg.* fighting (?); plunder (?) (18)

or-leȝe (-legu) *n.* battle, war, hostility: *aj.* hostile (24)

or-liehtre *aj.* blameless (57)

or-læȝ *n.sg.* fate (160)

or-mód *aj.* despairing (840)

or-mǽte *aj.* excessive (145)

oroþ *n.sg.* breath (13)

or-sáwle *aj.* lifeless (273)

or-scylde *aj.* guiltless (96)

or-sorg *aj.* untroubled (174)

ȝe-or-tríewan *I* doubt, disbelieve (74)

or-tríewe *aj.* despairing (74)

or-wearde *aj.* lacking a guardian (257)

or-wierðu *f.sg.* shame (227)

or-wíȝe *aj.* defenseless (231)

or-wœne *aj.* despairing (151)

or-þanc *m.sg.* mind, skill, genius; thoughtlessness: *aj.* ingenious, skillful (509)

or-þancum *av.dat.* skillfully (509)

ós (*gen.pl.* œsa) *m.* high divinity (?); first element in pers. names; name of long O-rune (6)

ostre (ostra) *f.* oyster (2)

oxa (~n) *m.* ox (2)

oþ *prep.cj.* to, up to, as far as, until (250)

~þe *cj.* until (250)

~þæt *av.cj.* then, thereupon, thereafter; until, so that (250)

oþ- *vbl.pref.* at, toward, beside; away, forth (250)

oþþe *cj.* or, and: oþþe . . . oþþe *correl.* either . . . or (221)

P

pád (~a,~an) *f.* outer garment, coat (7)

palma *m.sg.* palm tree (4)

ȝe-palm-twigian *II* deck with palm branches (4)

pandher (~as) *m.* panther (1)

panne *f.sg.* pan (1)

pápa (~n) *m.* pope (4)

péa (~n) *m.* peacock (1)

péo (~n) *f.* dog-flea, parasite (?) (1)

peorþ *m.sg.*(?) *meaning unknown*; name of P-rune (1)

pernex *m.sg.* a supposed bird (*from* Lat. *pernix*) (1)

pić *m.sg.* pitch, tar (1)

píl (~as) *m.* arrow, dart, spear (3)

plaster *n.sg.* (medical) plaster (1)

plega (~n) *m.* quick movement; sport; battle (30)

plegan (*def.*)5, plegian *II* move quickly; clap hands; play; fight (30)

port (~as) *m.* gate, portal (1)

portic *m.sg.* porch (1)

prass *m.sg.* proud array or bearing (?); tumult (?) (1)

préost (~as) *m.* priest (2)

pund (~) *n.* pound (weight) (2)

á-pundrian *II* adjudge, weigh out (2)

for-pyndan *I* do away, remove (2)

pytt *m.sg.* pit (1)

pæþ (paðas) *m.* path, route (17)

pæþþan *I* traverse (17)

Q

Q *the letter and the* cweorþ-*rune, meaning unknown* (1)

R

raca (~n) *m.* messenger (76)

racente (racentan) *f.* bond, chain (8)

racentéag *f.sg.* bond, chain (8)

racian *II* arrange, rule, govern (76)

racu (raca) *f.* (orderly) narration; course; channel (76)

rád (~a) *f.* riding, raid, journey, way; sea (as a roadstead or riding place for what swims or floats?); sound, modulation, music; name of R-rune (56)

rád *see* rídan

ȝe-rád *aj.* conditioned, prepared; apt, skillful (174)

~scipe *m.sg.* discretion (340)

rade/raðe *av.* quickly (128)

ramm (~as) *m.* ram, male sheep (5)

ranc *aj.* bold; straight (1)

rand (~as) *m.* boss, border, rim; shield (37)

~burg (-byriʒ) *f.* fortified town; shield-wall (of waves) (398)

rann *see* rínnan

ráp (~as) *m.* rope, bond (14)

rás *see* rísan

rásettan *I* move impetuously, rage (2)

rásian *II* explore, search out, ransack: a~ detect, seize (4)

réac *see* réocan

réad, ~e, *aj.av.* red(ly); in red (35)

réad *see* réodan

réaf (~) *n.* plunder; garment (65)

~lác *f.n.sg.* robbery (200)

réafere *m.sg.* robber (65)

réafian *II* plunder, ravage: á~ tear apart, separate (?): be~ deprive, rob (65)

ʒe-rec *n.sg.* rule, decree (76)

~líċe *av.* directly (322)

reċċan (reahte) *I* expound, teach; speak; direct, rule: á~ expound, teach, relate; reach out, put forth; raise up (76)

reċċan (róhte) *I* care, trouble about (19)

reċċend (~) *m.* guide, ruler (76)

reċed (~as) *m.* hall, house (42)

recen, ~e *aj.av.* quick(ly) (65)

ʒe-recenian *II* explain (1)

redian (?) *II* make ready: á~ prepare, find, reach (3)

rédon *see* rǽdan

reðran (?) *I* make ready, prepare (1)

reʒn (~as) *m.* rain (31)

~iʒ *aj.* rainy (31)

reʒn- *intensive pref.* very, very great, mighty (13)

~heard *aj.* wondrously strong (261)

~þéof (~as) *m.* arch-thief (7)

ʒe-reʒne (-reʒnu) *n.* ornament (13)

reʒnian *II* prepare, establish, adorn (13)

regol (~as) *m.* rule, canon (2)

ren (~as) *m.* house, hall (18)

to-rendan *I* rend, tear apart (1)

réoc *aj.* wild, fierce (1)

réocan (éa, u, o) *2* smoke; reek (17)

réod *aj.* red, ruddy (35)

réodan (éa, u, o) *2* redden (35)

reodian *II* arrange (?); pursue (?); sift (?) (1)

réofan (éa, u, o) *2* break, rend, rive: be~ rob, bereave (8)

réoh *aj.* rough (11)

réoniʒ *aj.* mornful, sad (7)

reord (~e) *f.n.* voice, language, speech (79)

~berend (~) *m.* human being (652)

reord.*f.sg.* food (1)

reord *see* rǽdan

ʒe-reord(e) (-reordu) *n.* food, sustenance; feast (79)

reordian *II* speak (79)

ʒe-reord(i)an *I–II* prepare, partake of food (79)

réotan (éa, u, o) *2* weep, lament: be~ bewail: wiþ~ abhor, oppose (8)

réotiʒ *aj.* tearful, sad (8)

réow *aj.* cruel, fierce, wild (11)

réowon *see* rówan

rest *see* ræst

restan *I* repose, rest; cease (93)

réstan *I* exult (?) (1)

ribb (~) *n.* rib (4)

-ríċ *m.suff.* (*in pers. names*) rich, mighty, powerful (486)

ríċe (ríċu) *n.* dominion, realm: *aj.* rich, powerful (486)

rícsian *II* rule (486)

rídan (á, i, i) *1* ride; rock, ride (at anchor); float, sail; hang; swing; oppress by swinging, chafe: ʒe~ ride up to; move: oþ~ ride, proceed (56)

rídend (~) *m.* rider (56)

ríeċ (~as) *m.* smoke (17)

ríeċan *I* smoke (17)

ríeċels *m.sg.* incense (17)

ríećen *aj.* smoky (17)

be-ríefan *I* rob, deprive of (65)

ríepan *I* pull, tear, rip (2)

ríerić (∼) *n.* reed (1)

rift(e) *n.sg.* clothing, cloak (1)

riʒnan *I* cause to rain (31)

riht (∼) *n.* right, due; law, justice, truth; account, reckoning: *aj.* right, straight, correct, just (417)

∼scytte *aj.* straight of aim (39)

∼wís *aj.* righteous, just (764)

rihtan *I* straighten; direct (417)

rihte *av.* rightly, justly (417)

ʒe-rihte (-rihtu) *n.* straight direction (417)

rihtend (∼) *m.* director, ruler (417)

rím (∼) *n.* number, count, reckoning (119)

ríman *I* count, enumerate, reckon (119)

rinc (∼as) *m.* warrior, man (102)

rind (∼a) *f.* rind, crust (2)

rinnan (a, u, u) *3* run; flow: á∼ run out: be∼ flow over, cover: ʒe∼ coagulate (41)

rip (∼u) *n.* harvest (4)

ripan (á, i, i) *1 (with aor. pres.)* reap, harvest (4)

rísan (á, i, i) *1* rise, rise up, get up (120)

ʒe-rísan (á, i, i) *1* be fitting, suitable (17)

ʒe-risne *aj.* fitting, suitable (17)

ríþ (ríðas) *m.* stream (1)

rocen *see* réocan

rocettan *I* belch forth; utter (2)

ród (∼a) *f.* rod; cross, Holy Rood (49)

roden *see* réodan

rodor (∼as) *m.* sky, heavens, firmament (146)

róf (∼) *n.* number, series (5)

róf *aj.* bold, strong; renowned (101)

rofen *see* réofan

rógian *II* flourish, bloom (1)

rómian *II* strive after, try to obtain (1)

róse (rósan) *f.* rose (bush) (3)

rót *aj.* cheerful (9)

roten *see* réotan

rów *f.sg.* quiet, rest (1)

rówan (éo, éo, ó) *7* row; sail; swim (4)

rówend (∼) *m.* sailor (4)

rucon *see* réocan

rudon *see* réodan

rúh *aj.* rough, hairy (2)

rúm *m.sg.* room, space, opportunity: *aj.* large, spacious, roomy (81)

∼gál *aj.* rejoicing in space (38)

∼heort *aj.* generous, noble-spirited (242)

∼líće *av.* abundantly: ʒe∼ at great distance, far off (322)

ʒe-rúm(a) *m.n.sg.* space (81)

rúme *av.* far, far away, widely; amply, liberally (81)

ʒe-rúme *aj.* expanded; manifest (81)

rún (∼a) *f.* secret, mystery, rune; runic, secret (or holy) writing (or reading); counsel, consultation (78)

∼stæf (-stafas) *m.* runic letter, rune (40)

∼wita (∼n) *m.* counselor (764)

rúnian *II* whisper (78)

runnon *see* rinnan

rúst *m.sg.* rust (1)

ʒe-rýde *aj.* pleasant; ready (2)

rýman *I* make room for, prepare; make way for, clear away; grant, allow (81)

rýn (rýde) *I* roar, rage (2)

ryne (rynas) *m.* running, flow, course, orbit (41)

∼ʒiest *m.sg.* swift foe (lightning) (51)

∼þrág (∼a) *f.* time of wandering (57)

rýne (rýnu) *n.* mystery, secret (78)

∼mann (-menn) *m.* one skilled in mysteries (1030)

rynel (∼as) *m.* runner (41)

ryniʒ *aj.* running, flowing (41)

rýniʒ *aj.* good in council (78)

rǽćan (rǽhte) *I* reach (out), extend; reach, attain, hit (23)

rǽd (∼as) *m.* advice, counsel, authority; (good) plan, wisdom; benefit, gain; power, might (174)

rǽdan (reord/rǽdde) *7-I* advise, arrange, counsel, instruct; conjecture; control, possess, rule: á~ arrange, determine; "read," decipher: be~ deprive of, rob: ȝe~ prepare; decide, determine (174)

ræde *aj.* prepared, ready (174)

ȝe-rǽde (~) *n.* armor, trappings; agency, equipage (?) (174)

rǽdelle (rǽdellan) *f.* riddle (174)

-rǽden *f.suff.* state, condition, terms, arrangement; rule, direction (174)

rǽdend (~) *m.* adviser, ruler (174)

rǽðe *aj.av.* quick(ly) (128)

ræfn(i)an *I-II* accomplish; endure, support (9)

ræft (?) *m.sg.* mold (?) (1)

ræȝ-hár *aj.* grey with lichen (1)

á-rǽman *I* raise oneself, rise (2)

rǽpan *I* tie with a rope (14)

rǽpling (~as) *m.* a bound prisoner (14)

rǽran *I* raise, erect; exalt (120)

rǽs (~as) *m.* rush, onslaught; leap (37)

rǽs (*instr.pl.* ~wum) *f.* counsel (174)

rǽsan *I* make a rush, attack (37)

ræscettan *I* crackle, sparkle (1)

rǽsele (rǽselan) *f.* conjecture, guess (174)

ræst/rest (~a) *f.* resting place, rest, repose (93)

rǽswa (~n) *m.* prince, leader (174)

rœ́ćan (róhte) *I* care, trouble about (19)

rœ́će-líest *f.sg.* carelessness, neglect (19)

rœ́ðe *aj.* just, righteous (174)

rœ́ðe *aj.av.* angry, cruel, fierce; harshly, fiercely (50)

rœ́ðiȝ *aj.* fierce (50)

ȝe-rœ́fa (~n) *m.* government official, prefect (5)

rœ́tan *I* gladden, make cheerful (9)

rœ́tu (rœ́ta) *f.* joy (9)

S

ȝe-saca (~n) *m.* adversary (466)

sacan (6, 6, a) *6* struggle, fight: for~ forsake, refuse: on~ resist, oppose;

deny, contradict: wiþ~ oppose; deny; refuse, renounce (466)

sácerd (~as) *m.* priest (14)

sacu (saca) *f.* strife (466)

sáda (~n) *m.* snare, cord (3)

ȝe-sadian *II* be sated, wearied (10)

sadol (~as) *m.* saddle (2)

~beorht *aj.* with brightly adorned saddle (242)

ság (?) *n.sg.* curve, depression (?) (27)

ság *see* sígan

ságol (?) (~as) *m.* stick, pole (?) (1)

sagu (saga) *f.* story, tale (380)

sál (~as) *m.* rope, bond (24)

salore *see* sæl

salu *aj.* dark, dusky (19)

salwed *aj.* darkened, blackened (with tar) (19)

salwiȝ- *pref.* dark (19)

sam- *pref.* together (221)

~heort *aj.* of one heart, unanimous (242)

~rád *aj.* harmonious (56)

~tenȝes *av.* continually (25)

~wist *m.f.sg.* cohabitation; matrimony (4189)

sám- *pref.* half-, imperfect (9)

~wís *aj.* dull, foolish (764)

~worht *aj.* unfinished (538)

same *av.* likewise (32)

-samne *aj.suff.* together (221)

samnian *II* bring together, assemble, gather (221)

samnung (~a) *f.* assembly (221)

samnunga/semninga *av.* forthwith (221)

samod *av.prep.* together, also; likewise; at the same time as, just as (221)

sanc *see* sincan

sanct (~as) *m.* saint: *aj.* sainted, holy (8)

sand *f.sg.* mission, sending (158)

sand (~) *n.* sand; beach (27)

~hof *n.sg.* barrow, grave (51)

sang (~as) *m.* song, poem; cry (149)

sang *see* singan

sangere *m.sg.* poet, singer (149)

á-sánian *II* droop, flag (12)

sann *see* sinnan

sár (~) *n.* sorrow; pain; wound (150)

~iʒ *aj.* painful; sad (150)

~stæf (-stafas) *m.* malicious reproach (40)

sár, ~e *aj.av.* painful(ly), grievous(ly); very (150)

sárgung *f.sg.* grief, lamentation (150)

sáriʒian *II* suffer, grieve; wound (150)

sáwan (éo, éo, á) *7* sow, scatter (12)

sáwol (sáwla) *f.* soul; life; living being (273)

sáwon *see* séon

scacan (scóc, ó, æ) *6* depart; hasten: á~ shake, brandish: on~ shake (26)

scád/scéad (~) *n.* distinction; discernment, understanding (39)

scáda *m.sg.* crown of the head (39)

scádan (é, é, á) *7* divide, distinguish between, judge: á~ separate, keep apart; hold aloof: for~ condemn (?); disperse: ʒe~ rule over (?); judge, decide, settle: to~ separate, split; decide (39)

scáden-mǽl *n.sg.* sword with a distinguishing design (57)

ʒe-scád-líce *av.* reasonably (39)

scadu (scadwa) *f.* shade, shadow (21)

be-scádwian *II* overshadow (21)

ʒe-scád-wís *aj.* discriminating (764)

scamian *II* be ashamed; blush; shame (42)

scamol *m.sg.* stool, bench (1)

scamu (scama) *f.* shame, embarrassment; genitals (42)

scán *see* scínan

scanca (~n) *m.* shank, leg bone (2)

scand (~a) *f.* disgrace, shame; confusion (26)

scea- *see also* scæ-

ʒe-scéad *see* ʒe-scád

scéaf (~as) *m.* sheaf of grain (3)

scéaf *see* scúfan

sceal *see* sculan

scealc (~as) *m.* servant, minister, man (34)

scéam (~as) *m.* grey or white horse (39)

scéap (~) *n.* sheep (13)

sceard *aj.* hacked, mutilated; deprived of, cut off from (52)

scearn *n.sg.* dung, dirt (1)

scearp, ~e *aj.av.* sharp(ly), keen(ly) (of materials, wit, vision) (38)

scearu (sceara) *f.* share, portion, division (52)

scéat (~as) *m.* corner, fold, place of concealment; lap, bosom (of the body); region, surface (of the earth) (40)

scéat *see* scéotan

scéawend-wíse *f.sg.* jesting song (764)

scéawere *m.sg.* observer (71)

scéawian *II* look (at), inspect, regard: be~ watch, consider, look to: ʒe~ see, consider, examine; show, display: ʒeond~ look upon (71)

scéawung (~a) *f.* inspection; spectacle (71)

scéaþ *see* scǽþ

scéd *see* scádan

scenć (~a) *f.* cup (4)

scenćan *I* pour out, give to drink: be~ pour over, cover (4)

scendan *I* put to shame, disgrace (26)

scenn (~) *n.* sword-guard (?); thin metal plate on sword-handle (?) (1)

ʒe-scentu (-scenta) *f.* confusion, shame (26)

scéoh *aj.* shy; frightened; wanton (?) (2)

scéon (scéode) *I* befall, happen; go quickly; give (6)

sceorp (~) *n.* clothing (8)

scéot *m.sg.* quick movement: *aj.* quick (39)

scéotan (éa, u, o) *2* shoot; shoot, rush forward, into: of~ shoot dead (39)

scéotend (~as) *m.* shooter, bowman (39)

ʒe-scíe *n.pl.* pair of shoes (3)

scieðede *see* scieþþan

scield (~as) *m.* shield; protection (38)

~burg *f.sg.* wall or roof of shields; place of safety (398)

scieldan *I* protect, shield (38)

scieldend (~) *m.* protector (38)

scielfan (ea, u, o) *3* shake (1)

scielfe (scielfa) *f.* shelf, floor (1)

sciell (~a) *f.* shell (2)

sciell *f.sg.* bloodshed (1)

sciell *aj.* sounding, sonorous (1)

scíene *aj.* fair, beautiful, bright (39)

-sciepe, -scipe *m.suff.* -ship; state or condition, skill or function (*of first element of compound*) (340)

ȝe-sciepe *n.sg.* what is destined, fate (340)

scieppan (scóp, ó, æ) *I-6* create, shape, destine: á~ create, originate: for~ transform: ȝe~ create; arrange; assign (340)

Scieppend *m.sg.* the Creator (340)

scieran (æ, ǽ, o) *4* cut, cut off, shear (52)

scierdan *I* damage, destroy (52)

scierian *II* set apart, allot, assign, ordain: á~ separate, divide: be~ separate from, deprive of; ȝe~ set apart, ordain; number, reckon (52)

sciernicge *f.sg.* actress, comédienne (1)

scierpan *I* clothe, adorn (8)

á-scierpan *I* sharpen (38)

scierpla (~n) *m.* clothing (8)

be-scierwan (æ, ǽ, o) *4* deprive (52)

-scierwen *see* ealu~, medu~

scieþþan (scód/scieðede, scódon, æ) *I-6* injure, harm (143)

scilling (~as) *m.* shilling, silver coin (2)

scíma (~n) *m.* radiance (14)

scímian *II* shine (14)

scínan (á, i, i) *1* shine (200)

scinn (~) *n.* phantom, specter, evil spirit (200)

scinnan *m.pl.* phantoms, specters, evil spirits (200)

scío *m.sg.* cloud (1)

scip (~u) *n.* ship (32)

-scipe *see* -sciepe

scír, ~e *aj.av.* clear(ly), bright(ly) (200)

~ham *aj.* in bright armor (93)

scíran *I* make clear; say; settle (200)

scóc *see* scacan

scód *see* scieþþan

scofen *see* scúfan

scóh (scós) *m.* shoe (*in pers. names*) (3)

scolde *see* sculan

scolu *f.sg.* troop, band (10)

scop (~as) *m.* singer, singer of tales, poet (8)

scóp *see* scieppan

scoren *see* scieran

scort (*comp.* scyrtra) *aj.* short (57)

scot (~u) *n.* shot, shooting movement (39)

scot *m.sg.* trout (39)

ȝe-scot (~u) *n.* chancel, sanctum (39)

scoten *see* scéotan

scotian *II* shoot (39)

scrád (~a) *f.* ship (36)

scráf *see* scrífan

scrallettan *I* resound (2)

scráþ *see* scríðan

scrid (~u) *n.* vehicle, chariot: *aj.* swift (36)

scride- *pref.* striding (36)

scridon *see* scríðan

scríðan (scráþ, scridon, scriden/scriðen) *1* stalk, stride: to~ be dispersed (36)

scríðe *m.sg.* course (36)

scrífan (á, i, i) *1* prescribe, decree, sentence: for~ condemn, proscribe; bewitch by writing: ȝe~ decree; appoint (34)

scrift *m.sg.* father-confessor (1)

scrincan (a, u, u) *3* shrink (1)

scrind *f.sg.* rapid course (36)

scrúd (~) *n.* garment (3)

scrýdan *I* clothe, shroud, envelop (3)

scræf (scrafu) *n.* cave (18)

scua *see* scuwa

scucca (~n) *m.* demon, evil spirit (3)

scúdan (éa, u, o) *2* hurry (1)

56

scúfan (éa, u, o) *2* push, shove, thrust; go, move, wander: á~ drive out; go away: be~ thrust; hurl: for~ repel: oþ~move, fly away: to~ thrust apart, disperse; remove (29)

sculan (sceal, scealt, scolde) *prp.* be destined to, have to; be necessary; be in the habit of; shall (mandatory) (764)

on-scunian *II* shun, reject (2)

scúr (~as) *m.* shower, storm (of the elements, of weapons); cloud; disquiet, trouble (28)

~boga *m.sg.* rainbow (172)

~heard *aj.* hard in the storm of battle (?); very hard (?) (261)

~scadu *f.sg.* protection against storms (21)

scúra *m.sg.* rain-shower, storm (28)

scuton *see* scéotan

scu(w)a (~n) *m.* shade, shadow (16)

scyccan (scyhte) *I* persuade, tempt (2)

scyld (~a) *f.* guilt, sin (96)

~freću *f.sg.* sinful craving (18)

~iʒ *aj.* guilty, sinful (96)

~wreććende *ppl.aj.* avenging sin (187)

~wyrćende *ppl.aj.* evil-doing, sinful (538)

ʒe-scyldre *f.pl.* shoulders (3)

scyndan *I* hasten, speed (9)

ʒe-scyrtan *I* diminish (57)

scyrtra *see* scort

scyte *m.sg.* shot (39)

scytel (~as) *m.* arrow (39)

scyttels (~as) *m.* bolt (39)

scæcel *m.sg.* plectrum (26)

scæcen *see* scacan

scæd (scadu) *n.* shade, shadow (21)

scæden *see* scieþþan

scæða (~n) *m.* foe; warrior; injury (143)

scæft (~as) *m.* shaft (of a weapon) (13)

-scæft *f.suff.* condition, nature, state (*of first element of compound*) (340)

ʒe-scæft (~a) *f.* creation, creature; destiny, fate; condition, nature (340)

ʒe-scǽnan *I* cause to shine (200)

ʒe-scǽnan *I* break, wrench open (6)

ʒe-scǽp (-scapu) *n.* shape, form, kind; creature, creation; destiny, fate (340)

scæpen *see* scieppan

scær *m.sg.* death, slaughter (52)

scær *see* scieran

scætt (~as) *m.* property, treasure, tribute, money; a coin (12)

scǽþ/scéaþ (scǽða; scéaða) *f.* (sword-) sheath (5)

sě, sío, þæt *art.aj.pron.* the; this; that; that one (he, she, it, *etc.*): sě-þe *rel. pron.* he, she, it who (10458)

seah *see* séon

sealh *m.sg.* willow (1)

sealm (~as) *m.* psalm (12)

~fæt (-fatu) *n.* vessel of song, psalm (31)

sealma *m.sg.* couch, bed (1)

sealmettan *I* sing psalms (12)

sealmian *II* play an accompaniment on a psaltery or harp (12)

sealt *n.sg.* salt, salt water: *aj.* salt(y) (27)

sealu *see* salu

séarian *II* become dry, sere; wither (2)

searu (~) *n.* cunning, skill, art; device, trick, treachery; armor, trappings; fighting: *pref.* cunningly contrived (118)

~hwít *n.sg.* artificial (brilliant?) whiteness (32)

~nett (~) *n.* woven armor, corslet; net of treachery (35)

~sǽled *aj.* cleverly bound (24)

~þancum *av.dat.* skillfully, cunningly (509)

searwian *II* prepare, make ready; cheat, dissimulate (118)

séaw *m.sg.* juice, moisture (1)

seax (~) *n.* short sword, scramasax (9)

séaþ (séaðas) *m.* pit, hole; spring (of water) (17)

séaþ *see* séoðan

secg (~as) *m.* warrior, man (100)

secg (~as) *m.* sedge, reed (1)

secg (~as) *m.* sea (23)

secg (~e) *f.* sword (5)

secgan (sæʒde) *I* say, speak, announce, recite; ascribe to, accuse of: á~ tell, proclaim: ʒe~ say, speak, narrate: on~ offer, sacrifice (380)

secge(n) *f.sg.* speech (380)

ʒe-seddan *I* satisfy (10)

sefa (~n) *m.* mind, understanding, heart (141)

seʒl (~as) *m.* sail; curtain, veil; pillar of cloud (12)

~ród *f.sg.* yardarm (49)

seʒlan *I* provide with sails (12)

seʒn (~) *n.* sign, mark; military standard, banner (29)

seʒnian *II* bless (29)

seʒnung (~a) *f.* blessing (29)

seld (~) *n.* hall, dwelling (142)

~guma *m.sg.* (mere?) hall-retainer (152)

seld- *pref.* remarkable, rare (14)

~cyme (-cymas) *m.* rare arrival (544)

~líć, ~e *aj. av.* unusual; wondrously (322)

ʒe-selda (~n) *m.* (hall-) companion (142)

seldan (seldnor, seldost) *av.* rarely (14)

sele (~) *m.* hall, house, dwelling (142)

~ʒe-scot (~u) *n.* tabernacle (39)

self *pron.* him-, her-, itself, *etc.* (491)

~scæfte *aj.* not born of woman (340)

~ǽta (~n) *m.* cannibal (65)

ʒe-sella (~n) *m.* (hall-)companion (142)

sellan (sealde) *I* hand over, give, pass, pay: á~ banish: be~ surround, cover: ʒe~ hand over, give, give up: ymb~ surround (276)

sellend (~as) *m.* giver (276)

semninga *see* samnunga

be-senćan *I* cause to sink, submerge (14)

sendan *I* send; apply (something to something): á~ dispatch: for~ send away, send to death: ʒeond~ cover, fill with: on~ send away, send forth, give up (158)

séo *f.sg.* pupil (of the eye) (494)

séoc *aj.* sick; sad; corrupt (22)

séoðan (séaþ, sudon, o) *2* boil, cook; cause to well up; brood over (something): á~ purify (17)

á-seolcan (ea, u, o) *3* become slack, remiss (2)

seolh (séolas) *m.* seal (animal) (2)

séon [<*seohwan <*sehwan] (seah, sáwon/sǽgon, sewen) *5* see, look; find; visit: be~ look, look on, behold: for~ despise; renounce: ʒe~ see, perceive, understand: ʒeond~ look over: of~ see, understand: ofer~ look on, survey: on~ see: ymb~ look around: þurh~ examine (494)

séosliʒ *aj.* distressed, afflicted (32)

seotol (~as) *m.* seat, cathedra (495)

séow *see* sáwan

sépan *I* teach (3)

sess *m.sg.* seat, bench (495)

sessian *II* grow quiet (495)

set (~u) *n.* seat, residence (495)

seten *see* sittan

setl (~) *n.* seat; residence (495)

~gang *m.sg.* setting (of the sun) (264)

setlan *I* settle; place (495)

ʒe-set-ness (~a) *f.* foundation (495)

settan *I* set, place, establish: á~ set, place, establish; make (a journey); apply; take down; transfer: be~ surround; adorn: for~ place before, prefer: ʒe~ arrange, place, establish, create; accomplish; possess; compare; settle, sit down: ymb~ set around (495)

Settend *m.sg.* the Creator (495)

sewen *see* séon

ʒe-sewen-líć *aj.* visible (494)

sibb (~e) *f.* clanship; relationship; friendship; peace (122)

sibb *aj.* related, akin: *as sb.* relation, kinsman (122)

ʒe-sibbian *II* reconcile, conciliate; gladden (122)

siċettung (∼a) *f.* sigh (1)

síd, ∼e *aj.av.* extensive(ly), wide(ly) (132)

∼fæðme(d) *aj.* wide-bosomed, capacious (63)

síde (∼; sídan) *f.* side (132)

sídian *II*(*intr.*) spread, extend (132)

sidu *m.sg.* custom; morality (2)

síðian *II* journey: for∼ die (834)

síðra *comp.aj.* later (834)

sielfren *aj.* made of silver (43)

síeman *I* load, burden (1)

síen *f.sg.* sight; vision; spectacle (494)

ʒe-síene *aj.* visible, seen (494)

sierċe (sierċan) *f.* corslet, byrnie (9)

síere *aj.* dry, sere (2)

sierwan *I* plan, plot; arm, equip: be∼ plot; ensnare; deceive, defraud (118)

siex *num.* six (24).

∼ta *aj.* sixth (24)

∼tíene *num.* sixteen (24)

∼tiʒ *num.* sixty (24)

sifian *II* sigh, lament (8)

sifung (∼a) *f.* lamentation (8)

sígan (á, i, siʒen) *1* sink, decline, fall; move forward (27)

siʒe *m.sg.* sinking (of the sun) (27)

siʒe *m.sg.* victory (234)

∼fæst *aj.* victorious (372)

ʒe-siʒe-fæstan *I* be or make victorious (372)

siʒel *n.sg.* sun; name of S-rune (11)

siʒen *see* sígan

siʒlan *I* sail (12)

siʒle (siʒlu) *n.* sun-shaped decoration, necklace (11)

sigor (∼as) *m.* victory (234)

ʒe-sihþ (∼e) *f.* sight, vision; what is seen (494)

síma (∼n) *m.* bond, chain (1)

simbel *aj.* continuous (222)

simbel/simble(s) *av.* always (222)

sin- *pref.* continuous, perpetual; immense (24)

∼gál, ∼e *aj.av.* continual(ly) (18)

∼gála, -gáles *av.* continually (18)

sinc (∼) *n.* treasure; riches; jewel (82)

sincan (a, u, u) *3* sink (14)

sinder *n.pl.* impurities (in metal), dross (1)

singan (a, u, u) *3* sing; recite poetry: á∼ sing; complete a song: be∼ bewail: ʒe∼ sing (149)

ʒe-sinʒe *f.sg.* wife (24)

sinnan (a, u, u) *3* heed, care about (4)

siofoða *aj.* seventh (47)

siofun *num.* seven (47)

∼feald *aj.* sevenfold (27)

∼tíene *num.* seventeen (24)

∼tiʒ *num.* seventy (24)

∼wintre *aj.* seven years old (116)

siolfur *n.sg.* silver (43)

sioloþ (sioloðas) *m.* sea (1)

sioluc *m.sg.* silk (1)

siomian *II* rest, wait; lie in wait; hang, hover (15)

be-sion [<*síohan <*síhan] (*def.*) *1* run, stream (with blood) (1)

sionoþ (sionoðas) *m.* synod (6)

sionu (sionwa) *f.* sinew (5)

siow(i)an *I-II* sew, link (4)

sittan (sæt, ǽ, e) *I-5* sit, sit down: be∼ sit in council; beset, surround: for∼ delay, neglect; become feeble, fail: ʒe∼ sit, sit up; seat oneself; inhabit, possess: of∼ sit on, press down, oppress: ofer∼ refrain from: on∼ seat oneself; fear, dread: ymb∼ sit around, surround; reflect upon (495)

sittend (∼) *m.* dweller, inhabitant (495)

síþ (síðas) *m.* journey, course, way, arrival; enterprise, errand, exploit; experience, fate; occasion, time (834)

síþ/síðor *comp.av.* later, afterward (834)

∼dæʒ (-dagas) *m.* later time (502)

∼fæt *m.sg.* expedition, errand, course (17)

ʒe-síþ (-síðas) *m.* companion, retainer (834)

ʒe-síþ *n.sg.* company, retinue (834)

siþþan (*rarely* síþ-þǽm) *cj.* since, as soon as, after (834)

slaga (∼n) *m.* slayer (97)

slát *see* slítan

sláw *aj.* slow; blunt (1)

sléa (∼n) *f.* (weaver's) slay or reed (97)

sléac *aj.* slack, lazy (1)

sléan[<*sleahan <*slahan](slóh, slógon, slæȝen) *6* strike, slay, kill: be∼ deprive: for∼ destroy: ȝe∼ forge, smite, strike down; achieve, obtain by striking, by an attack: of∼ slay (97)

sléap *see* slúpan

ȝe-sleććan (sleahte) *I* weaken (1)

sleȝe (slegas) *m.* blow, stroke (97)

∼fǽȝe *aj.* doomed to be slain (51)

slép *see* slǽpan

slídan (á, i, i) *1* slip, slide (4)

slide *m.sg.* slip, error (4)

slidor *aj.* slippery (4)

slíðan *I* wound (11)

slíðe *av.* direly (11)

slíðe(n) *aj.* dangerous, cruel, hard (11)

slieht (∼as) *m.* blow, stroke; slaughter (97)

slíepan *I* slip, put on or off (21)

slincan (a, u, u) *3* crawl (1)

slítan (á, i, i) *1* slit, cut, rend, divide (30)

slite *m.sg.* cut, bite (30)

slógon, slóh *see* sléan

slopen *see* slúpan

slúma (∼n) *m.* slumber (2)

slúpan (éa, u, o) *2* slip, glide: á∼ slip away: tó∼ slip off, be relaxed (21)

slæȝen *see* sléan

slǽp (∼as) *m.* sleep, slumber (56)

slǽpan (é, é, ǽ) *7* sleep (56)

sméagan (sméade) *I* meditate, consider, reflect upon (12)

sméah *aj.* subtle, refined (12)

sméa-líće *av.* accurately, carefully (12)

smeoru *n.sg.* fat, ointment (4)

smicre *aj.av.* beautiful(ly), elegant(ly) (4)

be-smiðian *II* work in metal (25)

smiðu *f.sg.* the craft of the smith (25)

smíeć *m.sg.* smoke, vapor (2)

smierian/smierwan *I* smear, anoint (4)

smítan (á, i, i) *1* smear, soil (10)

smiþ (smiðas) *m.* artisan, smith (25)

smoca *m.sg.* smoke (2)

smolt, ∼e *aj.av.* peaceful(ly), gentle; gently (10)

þurh-smúgan (éa, u, o) *2* pierce through (2)

smylte *aj.* mild, serene (10)

smæcc (∼as) *m.* taste, flavor (1)

smæl *aj.* narrow, small, graceful (1)

smǽte *aj.* pure, refined (3)

smœ́ðe *aj.* smooth (5)

snáw (∼as) *m.* snow (18)

snáþ *see* sníðan

snell *aj.* active, quick, bold (21)

snéome *av.* quickly (37)

snéowan (ó, ó, éo) *7* hasten (37)

snícan (á, i, i) *1* creep (2)

sníðan (snáþ, snidon, i) *1* cut; reap (8)

snierian *I* hasten (3)

sníwan *I* snow (18)

snotor *aj.* wise, prudent (137)

snúd, ∼e *aj.av.* imminent; quickly (16)

snytre *aj.* wise (137)

snytrian *II* be wise, know (137)

snytru (snytra) *f.* wisdom (137)

snyþþan *I* hasten (16)

be-snyþþan *I* deprive (3)

snǽd (∼as) *m.* morsel, slice of food (8)

be-snǽdan *I* cut off (8)

snæȝl *m.sg.* snail (1)

snœr (∼e) *f.* string (of a harp) (2)

sóc, socen *see* sacan, súcan

sócn *f.sg.* visitation, attack; refuge (466)

soden *see* séoðan

sóðe *av.* truly, justly (513)

sófte (sœft, softost) *av.* softly, gently (29)

sogen *see* súgan

sól (∼) *n.* sun (2)

∼monaþ *m.sg.* February (30)

sól *aj.* dirty (19)

sólian *II* become dark (19)

solor *m.sg.* upper room, sollar (2)

sóm *f.sg.* reconciliation: ʒe~ *aj.* in agreement, peaceful (7)

sóna *av.* immediately (110)

sorg (~a) *f.* sorrow, anxiety (174)

~stæf (-stafas) *m.* trouble, affliction (40)

sorgian *II* sorrow, grieve: be~ regret; shrink from, dread (174)

sorgung (~a) *f.* grieving (174)

sóþ (~) *n.* truth, righteousness, justice (513)

~fæst *aj.* honest, just (372)

sóþ *aj.* true, real; righteous, just (513)

spáld/spátl *n.sg.* spittle (12)

spanan (éo, éo, a) *7* lure, lure on (15)

spang (~e) *f.* buckle, clasp (2)

ʒe-spang *n.sg.* buckle, clasp (2)

ʒe-spann *n.sg.* buckle, fastening, yoke (6)

ʒe-spann *n.sg.* allurement (15)

spannan (éo, éo, a) *7* fasten, tighten up: on~ undo, unfasten (6)

sparian *II* spare, protect (4)

spátle *see* spáld

spearca (~n) *m.* spark (4)

spearcian *II* throw out sparks (4)

spearn *see* spurnan

spearwa (~n) *n.* sparrow (4)

specan (æ, ǽ, e) *5* speak (2)

spell (~) *n.* statement, story, fable, discourse, message (66)

spellian *II* discourse; announce (66)

spellung (~a) *f.* conversation, discourse, narrative (66)

spéon(n) *see* spanan, spannan

spéow *see* spówan

spéowan *I* spit, spew (7)

spere (speru) *n.* spear (15)

for-spierćan *I* spurt until dry, dry up (4)

spild *m.sg.* ruin, destruction (7)

spildan *I* destroy: for~ disperse, waste (7)

spillan *I* spend, waste; kill (7)

spíwan (á, i, i) *1* spit, vomit (12)

spiwol *aj.* emetic; vomiting (12)

splott (~as) *m.* spot (1)

spor *n.sg.* track, course (21)

spornen *see* spurnan

sporu *f.sg.* spur, talon, claw (21)

spówan (éo, éo, ó) *7* prosper (137)

spówend-líće *av.* successfully (137)

sprang *see* springan

spréat *see* sprútan

ʒe-sprec *n.sg.* faculty of speech (249)

spreca (~n) *m.* speaker, counselor (249)

sprecan (æ, ǽ, e) *5* speak (249)

on-spreććan *I* enliven (?) (1)

sprenʒan *I* break, shiver, scatter (23)

spréot *m.sg.* spear (4)

ʒe-spring *n.sg.* spring; source (23)

springan (a, u, u) *3* spring, leap, jump, burst forth, fly: á~ dwindle, fail: ʒe~ spring forth, arise; originate, cause: on~ spring asunder; originate, bring forth: æt~ spring forth (23)

sproten *see* sprútan

sprungon *see* springan

sprútan (éa, u, o) *2* sprout: á~ sprout: ʒeond~ pervade (4)

spryńʒ (~) *n.* spring; source (23)

sprýtan/spryttan *I* sprout (4)

spræc *see* sprecan

sprǽć (~a) *f.* speech, utterance; narrative; judicial verdict (249)

-sprǽće *aj.suff.* of speech (249)

spurnan (ea, u, o) *3* kick, strike against (21)

spyrian *II* pursue; explore; explain (21)

spǽć *f.sg.* speech (2)

spǽtan *I* spit (12)

spœd (~e) *f.* speed, quickness; success, prosperity ; progeny ; abundance, wealth; power, faculty (137)

~iʒ *aj.* successful, prosperous (137)

~líće *av.* quickly, effectively (322)

spœdan *I* succeed, prosper, be wealthy: á~ escape, survive: ʒe~ succeed, prosper (137) staðol (~as) *m.* foundation, base, seat, station; firmament (80)

staðolian *II* establish, confirm (80)

stág *see* stígan

stal-gang (~as) *m.* stealthy advance (264)

stálian *II* establish (16)

stalu (stala) *f.* thievery, stealing (15)

stán (~as) *m.* stone; name of ST-rune (93)

~boga (~n) *m.* arch of stone (172)

~fág *aj.* decorated with stone, paved (42)

~ʒe-fóg (~) *n.* mason's art (21)

~gripe (-gripa) *m.* handful of stones (58)

stanc *see* stincan

standan (stód, ó, standen) *6* stand; remain; stop; start, continue; appear: á~ stand up, arise: be~ stand around, line, surround: for~ impede, prevent; withstand; defend, stand up for; understand: ʒe~ stand, stand fast; assail: of~ remain standing: oþ~ baffle, hinder, perplex: wiþ~ withstand: ymb~ surround: æt~ stand fast, be fixed (293)

stang *see* stingan

stapa (~n) *m.* walker, stalker (39)

stapol (~as) *m.* pillar; step, flight of steps (4)

starian *II* look at, stare at (13)

stealc *aj.* steep, precipitous (3)

steald (~) *n.* dwelling; possession (14)

stealdan *I* possess, own (14)

steall (~as; ~) *m.n.* place, position (16) (16)

ʒe-stealla (~n) *m.* companion (16)

steallian *II* take place (16)

stéam (~as) *m.* steam, moisture (11)

stéap *m.sg.* beaker, tankard: *aj.* high, towering (46)

stearc *aj.* strong; violent (15)

stearn (~as) *m.* sea-swallow, tern (genus *Sterna*) (1)

stede (~) *m.* place; military position (83)

stefn (~as) *m.* ship's prow; root, stem, trunk; race, people (118)

~byrd *f.sg.* control, direction (652)

stefn (~a) *f.* voice (118)

stefna (~n) *m.* ship's prow (118)

ʒe-stefnan *I* institute, regulate, control (118)

stefnettan *I* stand fast (118)

stelan (æ, á, o) *4* steal (15)

stellan (stealde) *I* place, put; á~ set, establish: on~ place, put; bring about (16)

stenć (~as) *m.* odor (27)

to-stenćan *I* scatter about, disperse (27)

stenʒ *m.sg.* bar, bolt; pole, stake (7)

stéop-ćild (~) *n.* step-child (17)

stéor *f.sg.* steering, guidance; penalty (13)

stéora *m.sg.* pilot (13)

steorra (~n) *m.* star (35)

steort *m.sg.* tail (4)

stepe/stæpe (~; stapas; steppan) *m.* step, going, gait, pace; step (of stairs) (39)

steppan (stóp, ó, æ) *I-6* advance, go forward, march, step (39)

stićel (~as) *m.* goad, spur (10)

stician *II* stick, stab; cling, remain fixed (10)

sticol *aj.* sharp, biting (10)

stíðe *av.* strongly, severely (47)

stíelan *I* temper, harden (10)

stíele *n.sg.* (low carbon) steel (10)

stíeled/stíelen *aj.* of steel; steely (10)

stiell *m.sg.* jump, leap (8)

stiellan *I* jump, leap, (8)

stíeman *I* wet (11)

stíep *m.sg.* fall, downfall (?) (46)

stíepan *I* elevate, promote in rank, advance (46)

stíepel *m.sg.* tower (46)

stíeran *I* direct, steer, guide; restrain (13)

stierć (~) *n.* calf (15)

stierćed *aj.* strong (15)

Stíerend *m.sg.* Guide, God (13)

á-stierfan *I* put to death (1)

stiernan *I* be severe (3)

stierne *aj.* stern, cruel (3)

stierninga *av.* severely (3)

á-stífian *II* be or become stiff, rigid (1)

stiʒ *n.sg.* sty; house, hall (2)

∼wita (∼n) *m.* housekeeper (?); house-
holder (?) (764)

stíʒ (stíga) *f.* path, way (152)

stígan (á, i, stiʒen) *1* go, move, set out,
step; ascend; descend (152)

stiʒe *m.sg.* ascent (152)

stihtan *I* arrange, order (4)

stihtend *m.sg.* ruler (4)

stihtung *f.sg.* arrangement, providence
(4)

stillan *I* be quiet, still; calm, appease
(45)

stille *aj.av.* still, fixed ; quiet(ly),
silent(ly) (45)

stincan (a, u, u) *3* move rapidly, rise,
whirl up; sniff (?) (27)

stincan (a, u, u) *3* stink; exhale: ʒe∼
smell (27)

stingan (a, u, u) *3* thrust (through),
stab (7)

stíþ *aj.* solid, hard, stern (47)

stód *see* standan

stofn *m.f.sg.* stem, branch (1)

stól (∼as) *m.* seat, chair, throne (51)

stolen *see* stelan

stóp *see* steppan

storm (∼as) *m.* storm; tumult; attack
(32)

stów (∼a) *f.* place (59)

strang (strangra, strangost) *aj.* strong,
severe, violent (148)

strange *av.* violently (148)

ʒe-strangian *II* make strong, strengthen
(148)

stréam (∼as) *m.* current, stream (128)

á-streććan (-streahte) *I* prostrate oneself
(1)

strégan/stréowian *I-II* strew, spread (7)

streʒdan (æ, strugdon, o) *3* scatter,
strew; fall (7)

strenǵ (∼as) *m.* bow-, harp-string; *pl.*
ship's rigging (5)

strenǵe (strenǵra, strenǵest) *aj.* strong,
severe, violent (148)

strenǵel *m.sg.* (powerful) chieftain (148)

strenǵ-líć *aj.* strong (322)

strenǵu (strenǵe) *f.* strength (148)

strengþ(u) *f.sg.* strength (148)

ʒe-stréon (∼) *n.* acquisition, treasure
(38)

stré(o)wen (stréona) *f.* bed, resting
place, hiding place (7)

stréowian *see* strégan

be-streþþan *I* bestrew, bedeck (2)

strícan (á, i, i) *1* move, go (1)

stríenan *I* acquire, get: á∼ beget: ʒe∼
acquire; beget; acquire, win over (38)

stríend *f.sg.* generation (38)

stríþ (striðas) *m.* strife, war (2)

strúdan (éa, u, o) *2* plunder, disturb (10)

strǽc *aj.* hard (1)

strǽl (∼as; ∼e) *m.f.* arrow (21)

strǽt (∼e) *f.* paved way, street (21)

ʒe-stun *n.sg.* noise (11)

stuncon *see* stincan

stund (∼a) *f.* time, moment (26)

stunde *av.* forthwith (26)

stundum *av.dat.* at times ; eagerly ;
laboriously (26)

stune *f.sg.* nettle, genus *Urtica* (?) (1)

stunian *II* crash, roar (11)

styćće (styćću) *n.* bit, piece; short time
(2)

styrian *I* disturb, stir, move; treat of,
recite; exhort (?) (38)

styrman *I* storm, rage; cry aloud (32)

stæf (stafas) *m.* staff, stick, column;
stave, written character, letter (40)

-stæf (-stafas) *m.suff.* (*forms abstractions*)
(40)

stǽʒel *aj.* ascending, steep (152)

stǽl *m.n.sg.* place, position (16)

stæl *see* stelan

stǽlan *I* establish, found; blame; avenge (16)

stæl-ȝiest *m.sg.* thievish stranger (51)

stǽnan *I* set with precious stones (93)

stǽnen *aj.* of stone (93)

stæpe, stæpen *see* stepe, steppan

stæþ (staðas; staðu) *m.n.* shore, bank (17)

~fæst *aj.* firm, stable (372)

stæþþan *I* support (17)

ȝe-stæþþiȝ *aj.* stable, firm; staid, serious (17)

súcan (éa, u, o) *2* suck (1)

sudon *see* séoðan

súðan *av.* from the south (48)

súðerne *aj.* southern; Frankish (48)

á-súgan (éa, u, o) *2* suck (1)

suht *f.sg.* illness (22)

suhter-fædran *m.pl.* uncle and nephew (4)

suhterga *m.sg.* nephew, cousin (4)

suhter-ȝe-fæderan *m.pl.* uncle and nephew (4)

sulh *m.f.sg.* plow (4)

sum *aj.indef.pron.* one, some (one); a certain (one); a notable (one); anything; *pl.* some (137)

-sum *suff.* -some; partaking of the quality (*of first element of compound*) (137)

sumor (~as) *m.* summer (25)

sumsende *ppl.aj.* swishing (of rain)(1)

sun- *pref.* sunny; of or like the sun (105)

suncon *see* sincan

sund *n.sg.* swimming, capacity for swimming; sea, water (65)

sund *aj.* in good health, safe and sound, healthy (28)

sundor *av.* apart, aloof, separately, asunder; singularly (36)

~nytt *f.sg.* special duty (26)

sundrian/syndr(i)an *I-II* separate, part (36)

sungon *see* singan

sunna (~n) *m.* sun (105)

sunne (sunnan) *f.* sun (105)

sunnon *see* sinnan

sunu (suna) *m.* son (188)

súpan (éa, u, o) *2* swallow, sip (3)

súsl (~) *n.* torment; toil (32)

súþ *aj.av.* south, southern, southward (48)

~heald *aj.* inclining toward the south, southern (26)

~weardes *av.* directed toward the south (882)

swá *av.* so, as; thus, such, likewise, equally; exceedingly: *cj.* so, as; that, in order that; or; when, as soon as, as far at; since, although: swá . . . swá *correl.* so . . . as, either . . . or (1278)

swác *see* swícan

swaðrian *II* withdraw; die out or away; disappear; cease (15)

swaðu *f.sg.* track (18)

swaðul *m.sg.* heat, flame (7)

swáf *see* swífan

swámian *II* grow dark; vanish; cease (5)

swamm *see* swimman

swan *m.sg.* swan (6)

swán (~as) *m.* young man, retainer (1)

swanc *see* swincan

swancor *aj.* supple, lithe (3)

swang *see* swingan

swangor *aj.* heavy (1)

swápan (éo, éo, á) *7* sweep, swing; drive; rush: á~, for~ sweep away: to~ sweep aside (8)

swara (~n) *m.* swearer (96)

and-swarian *II* answer (96)

swaru *f.sg.* swearing (96)

swát *m.sg.* sweat; vapor; blood; labor, toil (30)

~iȝ *aj.* sweaty; bloody (30)

swealg *see* swelgan

swealt *see* sweltan

swealwe *f.sg.* swallow (bird) (1)

swearc *see* sweorcan

sweart *aj.* dark, black; gloomy; evil (79)

swearte *av.* miserably; evilly (79)

swebban (swefede) *I* put to sleep, put to death, slay (60)

be-sweðian *II* wrap up (1)

sweðrian *II* withdraw; die out or away; disappear; cease (15)

swefan (æ, ǽ, e) *5* sleep; sleep in death (60)

swefel *m.sg.* sulphur (2)

swefn (~u) *n.* sleep; dream, vision (60)

swefnian *II* dream (60)

sweȝel *n.sg.* sun; sky; heaven; melody (98)

~bósmas *m.pl.* heaven (20)

~rád *f.sg.* modulation, music (56)

sweȝle *aj.av.* bright(ly), clear(ly) (98)

swelan (æ, ǽ, o) *4* burn (7)

swelć *pron.* such, which (389)

swelće *av.cj.* as it were; likewise, also (389)

swelgan (ea, u, o) *3* devour, swallow (39)

swellan (ea, u, o) *3* swell (2)

swelling (~a) *f.* swelling sail (2)

sweltan (ea, u, o) *3* die (51)

swenćan *I* torment, oppress (36)

ȝe-swenćan *I* strike; drive; torment, oppress (36)

swenȝ (~as) *m.* blow, stroke (36)

to-swenȝan *I* scatter about, disperse (36)

sweofot *n.sg.* sleep (60)

swéog *see* swógan

sweoloþ *m.n.sg.* heat, flames (7)

swéop *see* swápan

swéor (~as) *m.* father-in-law (3)

ȝe-sweorc *n.sg.* darkness (17)

sweorcan (ea, u, o) *3* grow dark; become grievous (17)

sweorcend-ferhþ *aj.* somber (183)

sweord (~) *n.* sword (114)

sweorfan (ea, u, o) *3* rub, polish (2)

sweostor (~) *f.* sister (8)

ȝe-sweostor *n.pl.* sisters; brothers and sisters (8)

swéot (~) *n.* troop (6)

swerian (swór, ó, o) *I-6/4* swear;

declare (?): for~ make helpless by magic (96)

swícan (á, i, i) *1* go; weaken, give way, desist; escape; desert, betray, deceive: á~ abandon; provoke: be~ deceive, seduce; circumvent, evade: ȝe~ fail, deceive; desist, depart (77)

swicc *m.sg.* odor (3)

swiće *m.sg.* escape, end; delay; deceit, offense, snare: *aj.* deceitful (77)

swician *II* wander, depart from, wander about; be treacherous (77)

swicol *aj.* deceitful (77)

swíðan *I* strengthen, support: for~, ofer~ overcome (381)

swíðe *av.* very, much, exceedingly, strongly (381)

swíðre *f.sg.* right hand (381)

swíer (~as; ~e) *m.f.* column, pillar (14)

swíera (~n) *m.* neck (14)

swierd/swierþ *n.sg.* oath, swearing (96)

ȝe-swíeru *n.pl.* hills (5)

swífan (á, i, i) *1* revolve, move, sweep: on~ swing, turn against; divert, turn away: to~ separate (8)

swift *aj.* swift (23)

swiftu *f.sg.* speed (23)

swíȝe *f.sg.* silence: *aj.* silent (18)

swíȝian *II* be, become silent (18)

be-swillan *I* wash (1)

swíma *m.sg.* swoon, fainting fit (5)

swimman (a, u, u) *3* swim, float, sail (65)

swín (~) *n.* boar, swine; boar-image (4)

ȝe-swinc (~) *n.* toil, labor, trouble, misery (36)

swincan (a, u, u) *3* labor, toil, struggle, be weary (36)

ȝe-swing (~) *n.* swing, vibration; surge (of the sea) (36)

swingan (a, u, u) *3* beset, scourge, swinge oneself; chastise, afflict; beat or flap the wings (fly) (36)

swingel(le) (swingella) *f.* whip (36)

swingere *m.sg.* scourger (36)

ʒe-swinn *m.sg.* sound, melody (13)

swinsian *II* sound melodiously (13)

swiotul(e) *aj.av.* evident(ly), clear(ly), open(ly) (52)

swiotulian *II* reveal, make clear (52)

swipa/swipu (swipan; swipa) *m.f.* whip (8)

swipian *II* whip, lash, scourge (8)

swipor *aj.* cunning (8)

swíþ *aj.* strong (381)

~feorm *aj.* fruitful; violent (30)

swógan (éo, éo, ó) 7 sound, roar (25)

swol *n.sg.* heat (7)

swolgen *see* swelgan

swolten *see* sweltan

swór, sworen *see* swerian

sworcen *see* sweorcan

sworfen *see* sweorfan

swulgon *see* swelgan

swulton *see* sweltan

swummon *see* swimman

swuncon *see* swincan

swungon *see* swingan

swurcon *see* sweorcan

swylt *m.sg.* death (51)

swæcc (~as) *m.* fragrance, odor (4)

ʒe-swæccan *I* smell (4)

swǽðer *pron.* whichever of two (186)

swæf *see* swefan

swǽfan *I* move (1)

be-swǽlan *I* burn (7)

á-swǽman *I* wander (1)

swǽr, ~e *aj.av.* heavy, heavily; sad(ly) (14)

swǽs *aj.* one's own; dear; beloved (40)

~líče *av.* gently, in friendly manner (322)

swǽsendu *n.pl.* food, feast (4)

swǽtan *I* sweat; bleed (30)

swæþ (swaðu) *n.* track (4)

swóéʒ (~as) *m.* sound, melody (25)

swóéʒan *I* make a (pleasant) sound (25)

swóétan *I* sweeten, make pleasant (32)

swóéte *aj.* sweet, agreeable, pleasant (32)

syflan *I* provide with relishes, spreads; flavor (1)

sýfre *aj.av.* pure(ly), chaste(ly) (2)

be-sylčan *I* weaken, exhaust (2)

sylian *I* soil, pollute (19)

syll *f.sg.* sill, base, floor (1)

symbel (~) *n.* banquet, feast (29)

symblian *II* feast, carouse (29)

syndiʒ *aj.* skilled in swimming (65)

syndr(i)an *see* sundrian

syndriʒ *aj.* separate, single (36)

synʒian *II* sin, do wrong (218)

synn (~a) *f.* sin; crime; enmity (218)

~iʒ *aj.* sinful; guilty (218)

~rúst *m.sg.* moral canker (1)

ʒe-syntu (-synta) *f.* good health, safety (28)

sype *m.sg.* soaking, wetting (3)

sǽ (~s; ~) *m.f.* sea, watery expanse; lake (165)

~čierr (?) *m.sg.* ebbing, retreat of the sea (?) (71)

~ʒéap *aj.* broad-based for sailing (14)

~láf (~e) *f.* leavings, spoils of the sea; survivor of the sea (?) (78)

~weall *m.sg.* sea-wall; shore, sea-cliff; wall formed by the sea (92)

sǽčč *n.sg.* strife (466)

sǽd (~) *n.* seed (23)

sǽd *aj.* sated with, weary of (10)

sǽgan *I* cause to sink, lay low, slay (27)

ʒe-sǽʒed-ness *f.sg.* offering, sacrifice (380)

sǽʒen (~a) *f.* saying, traditional tale (380)

sǽgon *see* séon

sæl (*dat.sg.* salore; *pl.* salu) *n.* hall (142)

~wǽʒ *m.sg.* wall of a building (16)

sǽl (~e) *m.f.* time, occasion; prosperity, joy (86)

~iʒ *aj.* happy, blessed, fortunate, prosperous (86)

~wang (~as) *m.* fertile plain (76)

sǽlan *I* happen, come about: ʒe~ come about; succeed: to~ be unsuccessful; be lacking (86) sǽlan *I* tie with a rope, bind (24)

ȝe-sǽl-líċ *aj.* fortunate (322)

sælþ (~a) *f.* dwelling, house (142)

sǽlþ (~a) *f.* fortune, prosperity (86)

sǽmra (sǽmest) *aj.* inferior, weaker, worse (9)

sǽne *aj.* negligent, slow (12)

sæp *m.sg.* sap (of a tree) (1)

sæt *see* sittan

sǽta *m.sg.* inhabitant (495)

sǽtan *I* lie in wait for (495)

sóċan (sóhte) *I* seek, inquire; desire; go, approach, get, visit; attack: á~ seek out: for~ afflict, punish: ȝe~ seek, go; visit, attack; beset; appoint: ȝeond~ examine, search: ofer~ try too severely, overtax: on~ exact from, deprive of (466)

ȝe-sóðan *I* testify to the truth of, prove (513)

sóft *see* sófte

sófte *aj.* soft, gentle (29)

ȝe-sófte *aj.* easy to bear (29)

sóel, sóelest *av.* better, best: *cp.* wel, bet (100)

sóelra, sóelest *aj.* better, best: *cp.* gód, betera (100)

sóeman *I* conciliate, pacify, satisfy (7)

T

táċen (~n) *n.* sign, symbol; Sign of the Cross; evidence, token; marvel, wonder; heroic deed (77)

ȝe-táċnian *II* make a sign, betoken, show forth (77)

táċnum *av.dat.* clearly (77)

ȝe-táh (?) *n.sg.* doctrine, teaching (?) (95)

talian *II* claim, count; think, suppose (45)

talu (tala) *f.* count, number; speech, narrative (45)

tam *aj.* tame (10)

tama (~n) *m.* tameness (10)

tán (~as) *m.* twig, branch; twig used in casting lots (17)

tang *see* tingan

tapor *m.sg.* taper, light (1)

ȝe-táwa *f.pl.* gear, equipment (2)

téafor-ȝéap *aj.*(?) built with red stone arches (?) (1)

téag (~a) *f.* cord, chain (95)

teagor *n.sg.* tear (of the eye) (23)

téah *see* téon, tíon

tealt *aj.* shaky, uncertain (2)

tealtrian *II* wobble, stumble (2)

téam (~as) *m.* offspring, descendants; company, troop (13)

téar (~as) *m.* tear (of the eye); drop (23)

tela/tila *av.* well; properly; comfortably (64)

ȝe-teld *n.sg.* tent (10)

teldan *I* cover: be~ cover over, surround: ȝe~ cover over (10)

telga (~n) *m.* twig, branch (17)

telgian *II* put forth branches (17)

tellan (tealde/telede) *I* count, reckon; account, consider; recount, relate (45)

á-temian *II* tame, discipline (10)

tempel (~) *n.* temple (of worship) (21)

tendan *I* kindle; cherish (?) (1)

tenȝan *I* press toward, hasten: ȝe~ apply oneself, join (25)

ȝe-tenȝe *aj.* touching, near to (25)

tennan *I* coax, encourage (?) (1)

téoða *see* teogoða

teofenian *II* join, put together (2)

téofrian *II* allot, appoint (?) (1)

teogoða/téoða *aj.* tenth (5)

ȝe-téoh *n.sg.* matter, universe (?); apparatus (95)

téon [< *téohan] (téah, tugon, o) *2* draw, pull, lead; teach, bring up; go, proceed, undertake (a course or journey); bring forth: á~ draw out, pull up; treat, manage; go, move, climb: for~ seduce; cover, obscure: ȝe~ draw, drag; bring about; incite; teach; bestow, grant; string, play (a harp);

take to oneself: of~ deny, deprive of, withhold: ofer~ draw over, cover: to~ pull apart, destroy; þurh~ accomplish, effect: *cp.* téon *II*, tiohhian, tíon (95)

téon/téoʒan (téode) *II* determine, make, form, prepare; furnish, provide: ʒe~ determine; allot, assign: fore~ foreordain: *cp.* téon *2*, tiohhian, tíon (27)

téon (~) *n.* vexation, mischief, harm, damage (46)

téon- *pref.* injurious (46)

téona (~) *m.* vexation, mischief, harm, damage (46)

ʒe-téona (~n) *m.* spoiler (46)

téone (téonan) *f.* injury (46)

téon-tiʒ *num.* one hundred (24)

teosol (~as) *m.* die; *pl.* dice (1)

teosu (teosa) *f.* harm, injury (3)

teoswian *II* harm (3)

teran (æ, ǽ, o) *4* tear, rip (3)

tíber/tífer (~) *n.* sacrificial offering, sacrifice (15)

tíd (~a) *f.* time, while; hour; season, festival (194)

~dæʒ *m.sg.* lifetime (502)

~fara *m.sg.* timely traveler (the soul after death) (366)

~líće *av.* seasonably, opportunely, in good time (322)

tídum *av.dat.* at times (194)

tíeder-ness (~a) *f.* weakness (?) (9)

tíedre *aj.* weak, frail; cowardly (9)

tíedrian *II* grow weak (9)

tíeʒan *I* tie, bind (95)

tielʒ *m.sg.* dye (2)

tíema (~n) *m.* leader (13)

tíeman *I* beget (young), multiply (13)

tíeme *m.sg.* span, yoke; *aj.* fit, proper, suitable (13)

tíenan *I* injure (46)

tíen(e) *num.* ten (24)

tíer *m.f.n.(?)* distillation, drop (?), mass, heap (?) (1)

tierʒan *I* worry, exasperate (2)

tíerian/tíorian *II* become tired, weary (8)

tierwan *I* caulk, paint with tar (1)

tífer *see* tíber

tífrian *II* offer a sacrifice (15)

tiʒða (~n) *m.* receiver, beneficiary (8)

tiʒðian *II* grant, bestow; permit (8)

tiʒel(e) (tiʒelan) *f.* tile (2)

tiʒen *see* tíon

tiʒþ (tiʒða) *f.* assent, permission; boon, favor (8)

til *n.sg.* goodness: *aj.* good, apt, useful, excellent (64)

tila *see* tela

tilian *II* strive for; acquire, gain; provide (19)

till (~) *n.* standing place, station (2)

tíma *m.sg.* time (3)

timber (timbru) *n.* material, substance; building, structure (39)

timbr(i)an *I-II* build (39)

ʒe-timbru *n.pl.* structure (39)

timpane *f.sg.* tambourine (2)

ʒe-tingan (a, *def.*) *3* press upon (25)

tinnan (a, u, u) *3* burn (1)

tin-treʒ (-tregu) *n.* punishment, torment, torture (by burning?) (4)

tin-trega (~n) *m.* punishment, torment (4)

tiohh (~a) *f.* band, company, multitude (46)

tiohhian (tiohhode) *II* appoint, assign; consider: ʒe~ appoint, assign; decree: *cp.* téon, tíon (46)

tíon [<*tíohan<*tíhan] (téah, tugon, tiʒen/togen) *1-2* accuse, censure: ʒe~ bestow, grant: of~ deny, deprive of, withhold: *cp.* téon, tiohhian (46)

tíorian *see* tíerian

tír (~as) *m.* glory, honor; (unidentified) star or constellation; name of T-rune (64)

tŏ *av.* to; thereto; also, besides; too, excessively: *prep.* to, at, toward, into; by, from, at the hands of; (*with dat. of sb.*) as (1748) tŏ- *pref.* to, toward; (*with vbs.: intensive, perfective, often destructive*) (1748)

toga (~n) *m.* leader (95)

to-ȝeȝnes *av.* in opposition to, toward, again, in reply: *prep.* against, toward (29)

togen *see* téon, tíon

togian *II* pull, draw (95)

to-gædre *av.* together (86)

to-heald *aj.* inclined (26)

tó-hopa *m.sg.* hope (3)

ȝe-toht *n.sg.* expedition, battle (95)

tohte *f.sg.* expedition, battle (95)

tó-hyht *m.sg.* hope (126)

tóm *aj.* free from (1)

to-middes *av.* in the midst (192)

tord (~) *n.* dung (1)

torht *n.sg.* brightness (85)

torht, ~e *aj.av.* bright(ly), clear(ly), splendid(ly), illustrious(ly) (85)

torn (~) *n.* affliction, grief; anger: *aj.* bitter, distressing (45)

torne *av.* grievously; indignantly; insultingly (45)

torr (~as) *m.* tower, crag (20)

to-samne *av.* together (221)

tosca (~n) *m.* toad, frog (2)

tó-weard *af.* facing, approaching, impending, future (882)

to-wiðere *prep.* against (487)

tóþ (tœ́þ; tóðas) *m.* tooth (17)

trág *f.sg.* affliction, evil (5)

trág ~e *aj.av.* evil(ly) (5)

trahtere (trahteras) *m.* commentator (2)

ȝe-trahtian *II* expound; consider (2)

tréaf-líc *aj.* grievous (1)

tredan (æ, ǽ, e) *5* tread, step; traverse (37)

tredd(i)an *I-II* tread, step; investigate, examine (37)

trega (~n) *m,* misfortune, grief (4)

trem/trym *n.sg.* space, step (2)

á-trendlian *II* roll (1)

tréo (~; trĕowu) *n.* tree; the Cross; wood (as material) (56)

tréow (~a) *f.* fidelity, trust, truth; belief, faith, good faith, covenant; favor, grace, kindness (74)

tréowian *II* trust in (74)

tríewan *I* believe, hope, trust (74)

tríewe *aj.* true, loyal (74)

tríewþ (~a) *f.* truth, loyalty (74)

trod *n.sg.* track, footprint (37)

trodu (troda) *f.* track, footprint (37)

trum *aj.* firm, secure, strong (82)

ȝe-trum (~) *n.* force, troop, host (82)

truma (~n) *m.* base, root (82)

trumnaþ *m.sg.* confirmation (82)

truwian *II* trust, have faith in: ȝe~ trust; confirm (74)

trym *see* trem

ȝe-trym *n.sg.* firmament (82)

trymian/trymman *I* arrange, array; encourage, exhort, strengthen: ymb~ surround (82)

trym-ness *f.sg.* firmness (82)

træd *see* tredan

trǽde *aj.* firm to walk on (37)

træf (trafu) *n.* tent; building (7)

tú *see* twœ́ȝen

túcian *II* ill-treat (1)

túdor (~) *n.* offspring, progeny; men (47)

~spœ́d *f.sg.* fertility (137)

~téonde *ppl.aj.* begetting issue (95)

tugon *see* téon, tíon

tulge (tylȝ, tylȝest) *av.* firmly (1)

tún (~as) *m.* enclosed place; dwelling (53)

tunece *f.sg.* tunic, coat (1)

tunge (tungan) *f.* tongue; language (33)

tungol (tunglas; ~) *m.n.* luminary, star (47)

turf (tyrf) *f.* turf (15)

turtle *f.sg.* turtle-dove, European dove (genus *Turtur*) (1)

túsc/túxl (~as) *m.* tusk (3)

twá *see* twœ́ȝen

twelf *num.* twelve (24)

~ta *aj.* twelfth (24)

twéo (∼n) *m.* doubt; difference; separa-
tion (19)

twéo(ʒa)n (twéode) *II* doubt, hesitate
(19)

twí- *pref.* two, double (143)

twídiʒ *aj.* granted (1)

twiʒ (twigu) *n.* twig (8)

twíh *num.* two (143)

ʒe-twinnas, -twinnan *m.pl.* twins (3)

ʒe-twǽfan *I* separate, put an end to;
prevent, hinder, deprive of (10)

twǽman *I* part, separate; hinder (143)

twóeʒen (twá, tú) *num.* two (143)

twóen-tiʒ *num.* twenty (143)

týder-ness (∼a) *f.* branch, generation (?)
(47)

týdred *ppl.aj.* provided with offspring
(47)

týdr(i)an *I-II* produce offspring, be pro-
lific; nourish, foster (47)

tyht *m.sg.* instruction; march, motion;
expanse, region (16)

tyhtan *I* teach, persuade, incite, lead
astray: á∼ produce, kindle; lead,
allure: for∼ lead astray: ʒe∼ teach,
train: on∼ impel, incite (16)

tylʒest *see* tulge

for-tyllan *I* lead astray (1)

týn (týde) *I* teach (95)

týnan *I* enclose: á∼ exclude, shut off:
be∼ enclose: ʒe∼ enclose; bury: on∼
open; disclose, reveal (53)

ʒe-týne (-týnu) *n.* court, enclosed place
(53)

ʒe-tynʒe *aj.* eloquent (33)

tyrf-haga (∼n) *m.* sod (22)

tyrnan *I* turn (5)

týtan *I* shine (1)

tǽćan (tǽhte) *I* instruct, teach; show,
direct; commit (into someone's hands)
(24)

tǽcnan *I* mark by a token (77)

tǽcne *aj.* demonstrable (77)

tæfl *f.n.sg.* die; game of dice (4)

tæfle *aj.* given to gambling (4)

tæʒel *m.sg.* tail (1)

tǽl *f.sg.* disgrace; reproach; blasphemy
(30)

tæl (talu) *n.* number, order, catalogue
(45)

ʒe-tæl *aj.* quick (1)

tǽlan *I* blame, reproach; blaspheme (30)

tæppere *m.sg.* publican, tavern-keeper (2)

tǽr *see* teran

tǽsan *I* tear, wound (1)

ʒe-tǽse *aj.* suitable (3)

tǽtan *I* gladden, cheer (1)

U

úðe *see* unnan

ufan *av.* from above, above (57)

∼cund *aj.* coming from above, celestial
(55)

ufane *av.* above (57)

uferra *comp.aj.* higher; later (57)

ufe-weard *aj.* directed up, upper (57)

ufor *av.* higher; farther off; late, later (57)

úht- *pref.* of the early morning (15)

úhta (∼n) *m.* (pre-)dawn, early morning
(15)

umbor (∼) *n.* child (3)

un- *pref.* un-; very (?): (*negative, pejora-
tive, reversive; intensive* [?]) (570)

un-ága (∼n) *m.* non-possessor, poor man
(370)

un-ár *f.sg.* dishonor (172)

∼líć, ∼e *aj.av.* dishonorable; shame-
fully, cruelly (172)

un-á-secgend-líć *aj.* ineffable (380)

un-á-wendend *ppl.aj.* unceasing (213)

un-á-þréotend *ppl.aj.* unwearied, per-
sistent (6)

un-bealu *n.sg.* innocence (94)

un-be-fohten *ppl.aj.* unopposed (65)

un-be-þierfe *aj.* unprofitable, vain (152)

un-biernende *ppl.aj.* unscorched (145)

un-blíoh *aj.* clean, bright (16)

un-bryće *aj.* inviolate, unshaken (105)

un-brýće *aj.* useless (94)

un-brǽće *aj.* inviolable (105)

un-ćéapunga *av.* without payment or recompense (18)

un-cúþ *aj.* unknown; alien; uncertain; strange, uncanny; unfriendly, hostile, terrible (539)

un-cýðiʒ *aj.* ignorant (?); wise (?) (539)

un-cýþþu *f.sg.* unknown country (539)

un-dearninga, -dearnunga *av.* plainly, openly (50)

under *av.* beneath, underneath: *prep.* under, beneath, before, within; under shelter of, in the lee of; at the foot of, in the presence of; in the service of, under the rule of; to, under, to the inside of (340)

undern *m.sg.* morning, midday (9 a.m.– 12 m.) (1)

un-flitme (?) *aj.*(?)*av.*(?) undisputed (?); indisputably (?) (14)

un-for-cúþ *aj.* honorable; noble; dauntless (539)

un-forht *aj.* very fearful (?) (89)

un-forht(e) *aj.av.* fearless(ly) (89)

un-fremu *f.sg.* hurt, loss (282)

un-fyrn *av.* soon (81)

un-fǽle *aj.* wicked, unholy (43)

un-ʒéara *av.* not long ago; very soon (84)

un-ʒe-blyʒed *aj.* unfrightened, intrepid (1)

un-ʒe-léaf *aj.* unbelieving (79)

un-ʒe-líć, ∼e *aj.av.* different(ly) (322)

un-ʒe-medemod *ppl.aj.* immoderate; vainglorious (192)

un-ʒe-met *n.sg.* excess; immensity: *aj.av.* immense(ly): ∼e, ∼es, ∼um *av.* exceedingly (146)

un-ʒe-scád *av.* exceedingly, unreasonably (39)

un-ʒe-sǽliʒ *aj.* unhappy, unfortunate(86)

un-ʒe-þéod *aj.* disunited (460)

un-gléaw (?) *aj.* very keen, sharp (?) (107)

un-gníeðe *aj.* not stingy; generous (2)

un-grund *aj.* bottomless, vast (124)

un-grynde *aj.* bottomless (124)

un-hár (?) *aj.*very grey (?) (30)

un-híere *aj.av.* dreadful, uncanny, eerie; horribly, fiercely (19)

un-hléow *aj.* offering no shelter, unfriendly (61)

un-hlitme (?) *av.*(?) without casting of lots (?); involuntarily (?); disastrously (?) (20)

un-holda (∼n) *m.* enemy, devil (144)

un-hrór *aj.* weak, (rendered) useless (?); very strong, resistant (?) (43)

un-hýðiʒ *aj.* unhappy (3)

un-hǽlu *f.sg.* damnation (272)

un-land *n.sg.* false land, supposed land (231)

un-lustum *av.dat.* joylessly (118)

un-lǽd(e) *aj.* wretched (12)

un-murn *aj.* untroubled (39)

∼líće *av.* recklessly; without regret, ruthlessly (322)

un-myndlinga *av.* undesignedly; unexpectedly (419)

un-mǽʒ (-mágas) *m.* treacherous kinsman (207)

un-mǽle *aj.* immaculate (57)

unnan (ann, annst, úðe) *prp.* grant, allow, wish, be pleased: ʒe∼ grant: of∼ begrudge, deny (29)

un-ofer-swíðed *aj.* invincible (381)

un-orne *aj.* simple, honest (1)

un-riht (∼) *n.* wrong (417)

un-rím *n.sg.* multitude (119)

un-ríme *aj.* countless (119)

un-rǽd (∼as) *m.* folly; crime (174)

un-rǽden *f.sg.* criminal act (174)

un-scamiʒ *aj.* unashamed (42)

un-scende *aj.* blameless, excellent, noble (26)

un-scæðiʒ *aj.* blameless, innocent (143)

un-scæft (∼a) *f.* monster (?) (340)

un-sláw *aj.* not slow; active, quick, sharp (4)

un-sófte *av.* cruelly, harshly; with difficulty (29)

un-stenć (~as) *m.* stench, stink (27)

un-swíciende *ppl.aj.* undeceiving, unfailing (77)

un-sýfre *aj.av.* unclean(ly), impure(ly) (4)

un-sǽliȝ *aj.* unhappy, unfortunate; causing misery (86)

un-tíedre *aj.* firm, stable (9)

un-tíoriȝ *aj.* untiring (8)

un-trág-líće *av.* not deceitfully, frankly (1)

un-twéo *m.sg.* uncertainty (19)

un-twéod, -twéonde *aj.* undoubting, unwavering (19)

un-twí-feald *aj.* sincere, without duplicity (27)

un-týdre (-týdras) *m.* monstrous progeny (47)

un-tǽle *aj.* blameless (30)

un-wác-líć, ~e *aj.av.* strong(ly), splendid(ly) (30)

un-wearnum *av.dat.* without restraint, irresistibly (34)

un-weaxen *aj.* not fully grown; young (96)

un-wemme *aj.* unblemished, inviolate (63)

ȝe-un-wend-ness *f.sg.* immutability (213)

un-wered *ppl.aj.* unprotected (130)

un-willa (~n) *m.* displeasure (998)

un-wrecen *ppl.aj.* unavenged (187)

un-wǽr *aj.* incautious (140)

un-wǽstm-bǽre *aj.* barren, infertile (652)

un-wóéne *aj.* despairing (151)

un-þanc *m.sg.* displeasure (509)

un-þinged *ppl.aj.* unexpected (25)

upp *av.* up, upward, above (267)

~cund *aj.* coming from above, celestial (55)

~cyme *m.sg.* rising, source, origin (544)

~gang *m.sg.* rising (of the sun); landing, passage onto land (264)

~hebbe *f.sg.* moor hen or water hen (genera *Gallinua, Fulica*), so called from its uplifted tail in gliding (?) or in courtship display (?) (139)

~lang *aj.* upright (13)

~líć *aj.* upper, supreme, celestial (322)

~riht *aj.* upright (714)

~weardes *av.* upwards (267)

uppan *av.prep.* over, above, upon (267)

uppe *av.* up, above, aloft (267)

úr *m.sg.* aurochs, bison; (*for* feoh?) property, wealth (?); manly strength (?); name of U-rune (5)

úriȝ- *pref.* dewy- (5)

urnon *see* iornan

út *av.* out, outside, forth (231)

út- *pref.* out, away (231)

~fús *aj.* ready to set out (93)

~land (~) *n.* foreign country (231)

~lende *aj.* foreign (231)

~weard *aj.* striving to get out (882)

útan *av.* about, from without, on the outside (231)

~weard *aj.* outside (882)

úte *av.* outside, without (231)

uton *see* wuton

útor *comp.av.* beyond, outside; to a greater degree (231)

úþ- *intensive pref.* (10)

~genġe *aj.* fleeting, fugitive, not to be retained (264)

~wita (~n) *m.* very wise man, elder, scholar (764)

W

wá *m.sg.* woe, distress: *interj.* woe, alas (19)

wác, ~e *aj.av.* weak, frail, pliable, timid; weakly, slowly (30)

wác *see* wícan

wacian *II* keep watch (96)

wácian *II* grow weak, relax, fall away (30)

wacu *f.sg.* watch, vigil (96)

wád *m.sg.* woad, blue dye (5)

wadan (ó, ó, a) *6* proceed, go: be~ emerge: ȝe~ go, advance, journey; pervade: ȝeond~ go through (a subject), familiarize oneself with: on~ come upon, take possession of; penetrate: þurh~ penetrate, pierce (52)

waðol *m.sg.(?)aj.(?)* full moon (?); wandering (?) (1)

waðum (~as) *m.* billow, wave (4)

waðuma *m.sg.* billow, wave (4)

wáfian *II* be agitated, amazed, astonished; hesitate (9)

wág *see* wǽʒ "wall"

wagian *II* shake, move (3)

wala/walu (~n; wala) *m.* stem, root; base, foundation (?) (3)

walu (wala) *m.* tubular ridge of a helmet (1)

wamb (~a) *f.* belly, womb (14)

wamm (~as; ~) *m.n.* spot, stain, scar; evil, crime; damage, loss: *aj.* bad, sinful (63)

wammum *av.dat.* grievously (63)

wan *n.sg.* lack: *aj.* lacking; *pref. (privative, negative)* (49)

~hál *aj.* unsound, ill (272)

~hyʒd (~a) *f.* recklessness (571)

~scæft (~a) *f.* misfortune, misery (340)

wana (~n) *m.* lack; *indecl.aj.* lacking (49)

wancian *II* fluctuate, waver (3)

wancol *aj.* shaking, unsteady, weak (3)

wand *see* windan

ʒe-wand (~) *n.* distinction, difference (213)

wandian *II* hesitate (213)

wandrian *II* wander; circle, hover (213)

wang (~as) *m.* field, place, plain (76)

wange (wangan) *f.n.* cheek, jaw (76)

wanian *II* wane, lessen; lack (49)

wánian *II* lament, deplore (3)

wann *aj.* dark (40)

wann *see* winnan

wanung (~a) *f.* waning (49)

wánung *f.sg.* lament (3)

wár *n.sg.* sea-weed (3)

~iʒ *aj.* covered, soiled with sea-weed (3)

-ware, -waru, -waran, -waras *pl.suff.* dwellers, residents, nationals (*of first element of compound*) (140)

warian *II* be wary, alert; keep, defend; inhabit (140)

waroþ (waroðas) *m.* beach, shore (24)

~faroþ *m.sg.* shore-wave, surf (366)

wároþ *n.sg.* sea-weed (3)

-waru (-ware) *f.suff.* dweller, resident: *cp.* -ware (140)

waru *f.sg.* protection, custody (140)

wascan (éo, éo, a) *7* wash (1)

wát *see* wĭtan

wáwá *m.sg.* woe, grief (19)

wáwan (éo, éo, á) *7* blow (of the wind) (2)

wáþ *f.sg.* motion, journey, wandering; chase, hunt (5)

wéa (~n) *m.* woe, misfortune (59)

~láf *f.sg.* survivors of disaster; wretched survivors (78)

ʒe-wealc (~) *n.* rolling, tossing (of waves) (9)

wealca (~n) *m.* rolling wave, billow (9)

wealcan (éo, éo, ea) *7* roll, surge (9)

weald (~as,~a) *m.* forest; wood; foliage (9)

weald *aj.* powerful, mighty (526)

ʒe-weald (~a; ~) *f.n.* authority, power; possession, dominion (526)

~leðer (~u) *n.* reins, bridle (6)

wealda (~n) *m.* ruler (526)

wealdan (éo, éo, ea) *7* exercise authority, determine, control, rule (526)

ʒe-wealden *ppl.aj.* subject to, under the control of (526)

wealdend (~) *m.* ruler (526)

wealdende *aj.* powerful (526)

wealh (wéalas) *m.* foreigner, stranger; captive; Celt, Welshman (3)

~stód *m.sg.* interpreter (1)

weall (~as) *m.* wall, earthwork, rampart; cliff (92)

~fæsten (~) *n.* defending wall, bulwark (372)

~wala *m.sg.* foundation (?) (3)

weallan (éo, éo, ea) *7* well up, surge (130)

weallian *II* roam, wander (2)

wealwian *II* roll, wallow (1)

weard (~as) *m.* guardian, warden, protector, possessor; lord, king (257)

weard (~as; ~a) *m.f.* guardianship, keeping (257)

weard *av.* toward (882)

-weard *aj.suff.* in the direction of (882)

weardian *II* watch over, guard, keep, protect; hold, occupy, possess; govern, rule: lást ~ follow closely: swaðe ~ remain behind (257)

wearg (~as) *m.* outlaw, criminal; wolf (56)

wearm *aj.* warm (14)

wearmian *II* become warm (14)

wearn (~as) *m.* large number (of) (42)

wearn (~a) *f.* refusal; hindrance; rebuke (34)

wearnian *II* warn, take warning, be on guard (7)

wearnung *f.sg.* warning; foresight (7)

wearp *see* weorpan

wearp *n.sg.* warp, threads stretched lengthwise in a loom (100)

wearþ *see* weorðan

wéas *av.* by chance, accidentally (59)

weax *n.sg.* wax (4)

weaxan (éo, éo, ea) *7* grow, increase, become powerful, flourish: á~ grow, arise, come forth: be~ grow over, cover, surround: ʒe~ grow up, increase (96)

webb (~) *n.* woven work, tissue, tapestry (16)

webba/webbe *m.sg.* weaver (16)

webbian *II* weave, plot (16)

weċċan (weahte) *I* waken; call up, bring forth, produce; encourage, exhort; move, stir: á~ arouse, awake from sleep or death: to~ awaken, stir up (96)

wecgan *I* move, shake; be moved (34)

wedd *n.sg.* pledge, surety (7)

be-weddian *II* wed (7)

weder (~) *n.* (fine or bad) weather (36)

~burg *f.sg.* exposed fortress, town (398)

-dæʒ (-dagas) *m.* day of fine weather (502)

wefan (æ, ǽ, e) *5* weave (16)

wefl (~e) *f.* woof (16)

weʒ (wegas) *m.* way, route (209)

~bráde *f.sg.* waybread, plantain, *Plantago major, P. rugellii* (64)

wegan (wæʒ, wǽgon, weʒen) *5* carry; wear; move; have (feelings), show (qualities): á~ stir up, excite: for~ destroy, kill: to~ disperse, scatter: æt~ carry away (34)

ʒe-wegan (-wæʒ, -wǽgon, -weʒen) *5* fight (231)

wĕl (bet, sǽl; betst, sǽlest) *av.* well (better, best); rightly, fully, very much (266)

~dǽd (~a) *f.* good deed, benefit (530)

~hwá *pron.* each, every (521)

~hwelċ *pron.* everyone, each, any (477)

~hwǽr *av.* everywhere (136)

~þungen *ppl.aj.* accomplished; virtuous (52)

wela (~n) *m.* wealth, abundance (266)

weleras/welera *m.f.pl.* lips (18)

weliʒ *aj.* prosperous, rich, opulent (266)

weliʒian *II* abound, be prosperous; enrich (266)

wemman *I* defile, profane; abuse, revile (63)

wenċel (~) *n.* child: *aj.* feeble, weak (3)

wendan *I* wend one's way, go; turn, turn aside, change: á~ turn away; change; cease: ʒe~ turn, cause to turn, change: on~ change; return; turn aside, put aside; take away from: oþ~ avert; take away from (213)

wending *f.sg.* change (213)

wenn *m.f.sg.* wen, tumor, cyst (6)

~ċíecen (~) *n.* little wen (1)

wennan/wenian *I* accustom; entertain, honor (5)

wéod (~) *n.* weed, tare (3)

~monaþ *m.sg.* August (30)

wéolc *see* wealcan

weold *see* wealdan

wéoll *see* weallan

weolma/wealma (?) *m.f.sg.* choice, best of a class (1)

wéop *see* wǿpan

weorc (~) *n.* work, burden; misery, grief, sorrow (538)

~sum *aj.* grievous (125)

ȝe-weorc (~) *n.* a work, product of work, craftsmanship (538)

weorce *aj.* difficult, painful (538)

weorce/weorcum *av.dat.* grievously; with difficulty (125)

weorðan (wearþ, wurdon, o) *3* become, happen, get to be, arrive at; (*in pass. constructions*) be: for~ come to nothing, perish: ȝe~ become, be; (*imp.*) settle, suit, be agreed, seem fitting (882)

weorðian *II* esteem, honor; praise, exalt, worship; adorn, deck: ȝe~ honor, dignify, reward; adorn (227)

weorðung (~a) *f.* honor, distinction (227)

weorf (~) *n.* cattle (1)

weornian *II* become weak (8)

weorod (~) *n.* troop, warrior band, people (220)

weorod *n.sg.* sweet drink (mead?) (1)

weorold (~a) *f.* world; men, humanity; life, way of life; age, cycle, eternity (476)

ȝe-weorp *n.sg.* throwing, tossing, dashing, turbulence (100)

weorpan (ea, u, o) *3* throw, throw away, cast, fling: á~ cast out, throw down; reject, remove: be~ cover; surround; cast out: for~ cast out, reject; throw away, squander: ȝe~ throw down; hasten away: ofer~ cast over, sprinkle overthrow; stumble: to~ turn aside; scatter; throw down, destroy: wiþ~ spurn: ymb~ surround (100)

weorþ *n.sg.* worth, value, price; dignity, honor; ransom; precious object: *aj.* worthy, honored, valued, precious, dear (227)

~mynd (~u) *f.n.* honor, mark of honor, glory (419)

wéox *see* weaxan

wer (~as) *m.* male, man (311)

wered *ppl.aj.* clothed, covered; protected (10; 130)

were-feoht (~) *n.* defensive battle (65)

wergulu *f.sg.* nettle, genus *Urtica* (?) (1)

werian *I* defend, protect, keep; occupy, inhabit; forbid, ward off; restrain: á~ defend, protect, ward off: be~ defend, protect; restrain, curb, forbid (140)

werian *I* cover, clothe: á~ surround, enclose: ȝe~ cover over, clothe (10)

wermód *m.sg.* wormwood, *Artemisia absinthium* (1)

wesan, (ne) wesan (wæs/næs, wǽron/nǽron) *sb.vb.*(*def.*)*5* be, exist, become; not be: ȝe~ converse, debate: *cp.* bíon (4189)

-wesende *ppl.suff.* being (4189)

west *av.* west, westerly, westward (31)

~mest *aj.* westmost (31)

westan *av.* from the west (31)

wíć (~) *n.* dwelling place, settlement, home; camp, station, fortress (95)

wícan (á, i, i) *1* weaken, give way, yield (30)

wiććung-dóm *m.sg.* witchcraft (2)

wicg (~) *n.* steed (18)

~cræft (~as; ~a) *m.f.* skill with horses (223)

wícian *II* inhabit, encamp (95)

wíćing (~as) *m.* pirate, viking (95)

wicon *see* wícan

wíd, ~e *aj.av.* wide(ly), extensive(ly) (312)

~brád *aj.* ample, extended (64)

~fæðme *aj.* extensive, capacious (63)

~gangol *aj.* wandering (264)

~ȝiell *aj.* extensive; wandering (6)

~lást (~as) *m.* long way, road: *aj.* far-wandering (72)

~scofen *aj.* widespread (29)

~scop *aj.* ample (340)

~síþ (-síðas) *m.* long journey: (*as pers. name*) Far-Traveler (834)

wíde-feorh, -ferhþ *m.n.av.* long time; for a long time, always (325; 183)

widewe (widewan) *f.* widow (8)

wídl (~as) *m.* impurity, filth (4)

wídlian *II* defile, pollute (4)

ʒe-widre (-widru) *n.* (fine or bad) weather (36)

wiðer *av.* against: *pref.* against, opposing (487)

~breca (~n) *m.* adversary, enemy (105)

~bróga (~n) *m.* adversary, enemy (33)

~ćierr *m.sg.* reversal (71)

~mœdu *f.sg.* enmity; perversity (840)

~rihtes *av.* just opposite (417)

~steall *m.sg.* defenses, resistance (16)

~sǽćć *n.sg.* contradiction (466)

~trod *n.sg.* retreat (37)

~weard *aj.* obstinate, perverse, rebellious (882)

~weard-ness *f.sg.* adversity (882)

wiðre *n.sg.* resistance (487)

ʒe-wield (~) *n.* power, control (526)

ʒe-wieldan *I* rule, control (526)

wiell/wiella/wielle (~as; ~an) *m.f.* spring, fountain (130)

wiellan *I* roll, twist, wallow (1)

wiellan *I* well up, boil: á~ bring into commotion, boil: on~ cause to boil; inflame (130)

wielm (~as) *m.* boiling, welling, surging, gushing; current, flood; ardor, fervor (130)

wieltan *I* roll (1)

wierć *see* wærć

wierdan *I* damage, injure, destroy (13)

ʒe-wierðan *I* estimate, value (227)

wierðe *aj.* worthy, honored; valued, precious, dear (227)

wierʒa *aj.* accursed, evil (59)

wierʒan *I* abuse, curse, despise: á~ condemn, damn (56)

á-wierʒan *I* injure, strangle; corrupt (3)

wierʒen *f.sg.* accursed female being (56)

wierʒend (~) *m.* reviler, enemy (56)

wierʒ-ness (~a) *f.* abuse, cursing (56)

wierʒþu (wierʒþa) *f.* curse, punishment, damnation (56)

wierman *I* make warm (14)

wiernan *I* refuse, withhold; prevent: for~ refuse, deny, hinder; forewarn (34)

wierp (~as) *m.* throw, cast; blow, stroke (100)

wierp *f.sg.* change, reversal; relief, remedy (100)

wierpan *I* turn, change; recover, restore oneself; á~ cast out: ʒe~ recover, get better (100)

wiers(a), wierst, wierrest *see* yfel(e)

wíf (~) *n.* woman; married woman, wife (122)

ʒe-wif (~u) *n.* web (of destiny) (16)

wifel *m.sg.* beetle (1)

wíf-mann (-menn) *m.* woman (122)

wíʒ (~)*n.* combat, strife, war; force, valor; troops (231)

~hafola *m.sg.* war helmet (16)

~haga *m.sg.* battle-hedge, wall of shields (22)

wiga (~n) *m.* warrior (231)

wíʒan *1(def.)* fight (231)

wíʒend (~) *m.* warrior (231)

wíʒlian *II* divine, foresee (2)

wiht (~a; ~e) *f.n.* creature, being; thing; anything, something (245)

wihte *av.dat.* at all (245)

wíl-becc *m.sg.* stream of miseries (?) (1)

wilde *aj.* wild, fierce, untamed (39)

wildor (~) *n.* wild beast (39)

ʒe-will *n.sg.* will, wish (998)

will- *pref.* willing; pleasant, joyful; familiar (998)

~cuma (~n) *m.* welcome visitor (544)

~dæʒ *m.sg.* joyful day (502)

~síþ *m.sg.* desired, pleasant journey (834)

~ʒe-síþ (-síðas) *m.* familiar, dear companion (834)

~sum *aj.* desired, desirable; pleasant; willing, voluntary (137)

willa (~n) *m.* will, mind, determination, purpose; good will; desire, wish; delight, pleasure, joy; desirable thing (998)

willan (wille, wilt, wolde) *anv.* wish, be willing; be about to (998)

willen *aj.* willing, desirous (998)

willian *II* wish, desire (998)

willum *av.dat.* delightfully; joyfully (998)

wilnian *II* wish, will, long for (998)

wilnung (~a) *f.* wish (998)

wín *n.sg.* wine (59)

~burg *f.sg.* festive town (398)

winćel *n.sg.* corner (1)

wincian *II* shut the eyes, blink (1)

winciende *ppl.aj.* winking, blinking (1)

wind (~as) *m.* wind (72)

~ʒeard *m.sg.* home of the winds, sea (167)

~iʒ *aj.* windy, wind-swept (72)

~sele *m.sg.* hall of winds (hell) (142)

windan (a, u, u) *3* (*intr.*) turn, move, curl, fly, circle, wheel; roll; delay, hesitate; (*tr.*) wind, swing, twirl, twist: á~ remove: be~ wind around, encompass, enclose; héafe ~ bewail: ʒe~ wind, twist; go, turn, escape: on~ unwind, loosen; retreat: ymb~ wind, clasp around: æt~ escape (213)

wine (~; winas) *m.* friend; friendly lord (110)

winestre *f.sg.* left hand: *aj.* left (4)

winn (~) *n.* struggle, effort, toil; strife, war; profit, gain (207)

ʒe-winna (~n) *m.* adversary, enemy (207)

winnan (a, u, u) *3* strive, contend, fight; toil, work, endeavor; bear, endure: á~ acquire; overcome: ʒe~ strive, fight; conquer, overcome, destroy: ofer~ conquer (207)

winter (wintru) *n.* winter; *pl.* years (116)

~fyllaþ *m.sg.* October (232)

wíoh (wíos) *m.* idol, heathen fane: *pref.* (*in prop. names*) (25)

~bedd (~u) *n.* altar (7)

wír (~as) *m.* (drawn) wire (12)

wís (~e) *f.* affair, matter, thing, reason; manner, wise; melody (764)

wís ~e *aj.av.* wise, experienced, learned, prudent; wisely (764)

~dóm *m.sg.* wisdom (367)

wísa (~n) *m.* guide, leader (764)

wíse (wísan) *f.* manner, way, custom; affair, matter; circumstance, condition, state; direction; melody (764)

wísian *II* direct, point the way (764)

for-wisnian *II* dry up, wither, shrivel (4)

ʒe-wiss *aj.* certain (764)

wisse *see* witan

wiss-líć, ~e *aj.av.* certain(ly) (764)

wist (~e) *m.f.* existence, subsistence, well-being; food; feast (4189)

wiste *see* witan

wita (~n) *m.* one who knows, wise man; councilor (764)

ʒe-wita (~n) *m.* witness (764)

ʒe-wíta (?) (~n) *m.* associate, companion (?) (225)

witan (wát, wást, wisse/wiste) *prp.* know; feel: be~ superintend, watch over: ʒe~ know, find out (764)

wítan (á, i, i) *1* see, guard, keep; impute to, accuse, blame: ʒe~ contemplate, observe; depart, go, leave, die: oþ~, æt~ reproach, blame for (225)

wíte (~u) *n.* punishment, torment; trouble, disaster (116)

~hræʒl *n.sg.* penitential garment (33)

wítega (~n) *m.* wise man, prophet, diviner (39)

wíteʒ-dóm (~as) *m.* prophecy (367)

wíteʒian *II* prophesy (39)

be-witian *II* watch, observe; arrange, carry out (47)

wítnian *II* punish (116)

witod, ~líće *ppl.aj.av.* certain,

appointed, ordained; certainly, truly (47)

witt *n.sg.* intelligence, consciousness, sense, wit (764)

~iȝ *aj.* wise, sensible, conscious (764)

ȝe-witt-ness (~a) *f.* knowledge, testimony (764)

wiþ *prep.* against, at, opposite to; near, toward; in contrast to, in relation to: *pref.* against, away (487)

wlacu *aj.* tepid, cool (1)

wlanc *aj.* rich, splendid, stately, proud; glorying in; boastful; greedy for (?) (72)

wlát *see* wlitan

wlátian *II* gaze, look (218)

ȝe-wlenćan *I* adorn (72)

wlenću (wlenća) *f.* pride, pomp, arrogance, high spirits (72)

wlítan (á, i, i) *1* look, gaze (218)

wlite (~) *m.* countenance; beauty (218)

~andett *m.sg.* confession of splendor (56)

wlitiȝ *aj.* beautiful, fair, radiant (218)

wlitiȝian *II* become or make beautiful (218)

wlóh (~) *n.* fringe of a garment (3)

ȝe-wlóh *aj.* ornamented (3)

wóc *see* wæcnan

wócor *f.sg.* growth; offspring, progeny (96)

wód *aj.* mad, raging (8)

wód *see* wadan

woddor *n.sg.* throat (1)

wóh *n.sg.* iniquity, perversity: *aj.* crooked, wrong, perverse, evil (19)

~bogen *aj.* crookedly, evilly coiled (172)

wól *m.sg.* sickness, pestilence (1)

wolcen (wolcnas; wolcnu) *m.n.* cloud; sky, heavens (86)

wolde *see* willan

wollen-téar *aj.* with welling tears (23)

wóm(a) (~n) *m.* noise; terror (40)

wóp (~as) *m.* weeping, lamentation (56)

~iȝ *aj.* lamenting (56)

word (~) *n.* word, utterance (631)

~ȝe-mearc (~as) *m.* verbal designation, limitation (73)

~laðu *f.sg.* conversation (11)

~léan (~) *n.* reward for song (151)

~riht (~) *n.* statement of law or custom (417)

worden *see* weorðan

worðiȝ (worðigas) *m.* farmstead, estate (5)

wórian *II* roam, wander; roll in pieces, crumble (2)

worn (~as) *m.* large number (of) (42)

worpen *see* weorpan

worpian *II* throw (100)

worþ (worðas) *m.* farmstead, estate (5)

wosa (~n) *m.* being, man (as consumer of food; as warrior) (4189)

wóþ (wóða) *f.* voice, sound, song; noise (20)

~bora (~n) *m.* speaker, orator, singer (652)

wracu (wraca) *f.* persecution; pain; strife (187)

wraðe *av.* angrily, fiercely; bitterly, cruelly (110)

wraðu *f.sg.* prop, support (17)

wráh *see* wríon

wrásen (wrásna) *f.* bond, fetter (4)

wrát *see* wrítan

wráþ *aj.* angry, fierce, hostile, terrible; bitter, harsh, cruel, evil (110)

wráþ *see* wríðan

wrecan (æ, á, e) *5* drive, drive out; express (in words), recite (a poem); punish, avenge: á~ drive away; strike, pierce; utter, relate: be~ drive away, drive around: for~ drive away, banish: ȝe~ punish, avenge: to~ scatter, disperse (187)

wrećća (~n) *m.* refugee, exile; warrior (187)

wreććan (wreahte) *I* arouse, waken (187)

wreðian *II* prop up, support, sustain (17)

wrenć (~as) *m.* trick, ruse; modulation, melody (5)

wrenćan (wreahte) *I* wrench, twist; plot, intrigue (6)

wríd(i)an/wríð(i)an *I-II* put forth shoots, be productive (10)

wriða (~n) *m.* ring (28)

wríðan (wráþ, wriðon, i) *1* twist, bind (28)

wriðen-hilt *aj.* having a spiral or serpentine design on the hilt (11)

wriȝels *n.sg.* covering, veil (59)

wriȝen *see* wríon

wrígian *II* go, wend (3)

wrigon *see* wríon

wríon [<*wríohan<*wríhan] (wráh, wrigon, wriȝen) *1* hide; cover; close (59)

writ (~u) *n.* written document; Scripture (53)

wrítan (á, i, i) *1* scratch, incise, inscribe; write: for~ cut through (53)

wrítere (wríteras) *m.* writer, scribe (53)

wrixl *f.sg.* exchange (20)

wrixlan *I* change, exchange, barter; vary: ȝe~ give in exchange, repay (20)

ȝe-wrixle *n.sg.* change, exchange (20)

wróht (~as; ~a) *m.f.* accusation, reproach, slander; fault, crime, sin; contention, enmity, strife; injury; calamity (19)

~ȝe-tíeme *n.sg.* crime; guilt (13)

~stæf (-stafas) *m.* accusation (40)

wrótan (éo, éo, ó) *7* root up (2)

wrǽc *n.sg.* misery; persecution; exile (187)

wræc *see* wrecan

wrǽn-ness *f.sg.* wantonness (2)

wrǽst, ~e, *aj.av.* strong(ly), firm(ly), excellent(ly) (12)

wrǽstan *I* twist, bend (12)

wrǽtt (~e) *f.* ornament (53)

wrǽþ (wrǽða) *f.* wreath (28)

wrǿȝan *I* excite, stir up (3)

wucu (wucan) *f.* week (7)

wudiȝ *aj.* wooded, woody (90)

wudu (wuda) *m.* wood; woods, forest; tree; the Cross; ship; spear-shaft (90)

wuldor (~) *n.* glory, fame, honor, praise (424)

wuldrian *II* glorify; be glorified (424)

wulf (~as) *m.* wolf (104)

~héafod-tréo *n.sg.* outlaw-tree, gallows, cross (56)

~heort *aj.* cruel, savage (242)

wull *f.sg.* wool (3)

ȝe-wuna (~n) *m.* habit, custom: *aj.* accustomed to (238)

wund (~a) *f.* wound: *aj.* wounded (76)

wunden *see* windan

wunden-mǽl *n.sg.* sword with serpentine markings (57)

wundian *II* wound (76)

wundon *see* windan

wundor (~) *n.* wonderful thing, marvel, miracle (236)

wundrian *II* wonder, marvel at (236)

wundrum *av.dat.* wonderfully (236)

wundrung *f.sg.* astonishment (236)

wunian *II* dwell; remain; be used to: ȝe~ inhabit; remain; stand; be used to: þurh~ persevere, be steadfast (238)

-wuniende *ppl.suff.* -dwelling (238)

wunnon *see* winnan

wunung (~a) *f.* dwelling-place (238)

wurdon *see* weorðan

wurma (~n) *m.* purple periwinkle, purple dye (2)

wurpon see weorpan

(w)uton *adhortative aor. vb.* let us (go): *cp.* ȝe-wítan (225)

wylf *f.sg.* she-wolf (104)

wylfen *aj.* wolfish, cruel (104)

wynn (~a) *f.* bliss, joy, pleasure; name of W-rune (208)

~sum *aj.* fair, joyful, pleasant, delightful (137)

wyrćan (worhte) *I* work, labor; construct, form, make; do, perform, attain; effect: be~ work in, insert, adorn; surround with: for~ do wrong, sin; forfeit; obstruct, barricade; ruin, destroy: ʒe~ make, create; strive after, achieve, bring about, gain, win: in~ (on~?) control (538)

wyrćend (~) *m.* worker, doer (538)

wyrd (~e) *f.* fate, destiny, Providence; fact, event (882)

~stæf (-stafas) *m.* decree of fate (40)

ʒe-wyrd (~e) *f.* fate, Providence; state, condition (882)

and-wyrdan *I* answer (631)

-wyrde, -wyrdiʒ *aj.suff.* of speech, -spoken (631)

wyrðe *aj.* worthy, honorable, noble; dear, precious (227)

ʒe-wyrht (~u) *n.* work, deed; desert, merit (538)

wyrhta (~n) *m.* worker, maker, craftsman (538)

ʒe-wyrhta (~n) *m.* author, doer (538)

wyrm (~as) *m.* worm; reptile, serpent; dragon (75)

~fág *aj.* with serpentine decorations (42)

wyrpel (wyrplas) *m.* varvel, ring on a falcon's jess or leg-strap (100)

wyrt (~a) *f.* plant, herb; root (45)

~truma, -wala (~n) *m.* root (82; 3)

ʒe-wyrtian *II* perfume, surround with fragrance (45)

á-wyrt-walian *II* root out (45)

wýscan *I* wish (5)

wǽćan *I* weaken; oppress: ʒe~ afflict; exhaust: on~ mollify (30)

wæćće (wæćća) *f.* watch, vigil (96)

wæććende *ppl.aj.* vigilant (96)

wæcn(i)an (wóc, ó, wæcned) *I-II-*6 waken, be born, arise: á~, on~ awaken; revive; arise, spring from, be born (96)

wæd (wadu) *n.* wading place, ford; water, sea (52)

wǽd (~a) *f.* garment (28)

ʒe-wǽde (~) *n.* garment (28)

wǽden *aj.* blue, bluish (5)

wǽdl *f.sg.* poverty, destitution, beggary (21)

wǽdla (~n) *n.* poor person, beggar (21)

wǽða (~n) *m.* wanderer (5)

wǽðan *I* wander (5)

wæf *see* wefan

be-wǽfan *I* wrap, enfold (1)

wæfer-síen *f.sg.* spectacle, display (494)

wǽfre *aj.* wavering, shifting, uncertain (9)

wǽfþu *f.sg.* marvel, wonder (9)

wæg *see* wegan

wǽʒ (wǽgas) *m.* wave; water; sea (84)

~bora *m.sg.* wave-traveler (652)

~dropa (~n) *m.* water-drop, tear (9)

~holm *m.sg.* wavy ocean (42)

~fæt (-fatu) *n.* vessel of waters, cloud (31)

~sweord *m.sg.* sword with (wavy) damascened blade (114)

~þel *n.sg.* wooden ship (8)

wǽʒ/wág (wágas) *m.* wall (16)

wǽʒ (wǽga) *f.* weight, scales (84)

wǽgan *I* trouble, afflict: á~ annul, destroy: ʒe~ afflict; frustrate (6)

wǽʒe (~) *n.* cup, beaker (9)

wæʒn *m.sg.* cart, wagon, wain (34)

be-wæʒnan *I* offer (34)

wæl (walu) *n.* carnage, slaughter; number of dead; corpse (127)

wæl- *pref.* corpse, carrion, death, destruction, slaughter; baleful, deadly, murderous, violent (127)

~ćeasiga *m.sg.* carrion-picker (raven) (173)

wǽl (~as) *m.* eddy, pool; flood, sea (2)

wǽlan *I* afflict, torment (3)

wæl-rápas *m.pl.* deadly bonds (of the sea) (?); water-fetters (of the icy sea) (?) (14)

wǽpen (~) *n.* weapon (91)

wǽpned *aj.* male: *as sb.* a male (91)

~cynn *n.sg.* male sex (389)

wær *aj.* wary, prudent, cunning (140)

wǽr *f.sg.* faith, fidelity; pledge; trust; protection: *aj.* true, correct (140)

~genǵa *m.sg.* one seeking protection, stranger (264)

~loga (~n) *m.* liar, traitor, devil (210)

wærċ/wierċ *m.sg.* pain, suffering (538)

wǽron, wæs *see* wesan

wæsma (~n) *m.* courage, vigor (1)

wæstm *m.f.n.* growth, stature, form; offspring; plant, fruit, produce, abundance (96)

~bǽre *aj.* fertile (652)

wǽt *aj.* wet (19)

wǽta (~n) *m.* wetness, moisture, water (19)

wǽtan *I* wet, moisten, water (19)

wæter (~) *n.* water, body of water, stream, sea (168)

~scipe *m.sg.* water, body of water (340)

ȝe-wóéd *n.sg.* fury, madness (8)

wóédan *I* rage (8)

wóéde *aj.* mad (8)

wóéðan *I* assuage, calm (4)

wóéðe *aj.* mild, pleasant (4)

wóéman *I* sound, be heard, announce; reveal; attract, allure; comfort, console (40)

wóémend *m.sg.* one who reveals (40)

wóén (~a) *f.* expectation, hope; probability; belief, opinion (151)

wóéna (~n) *m.* hope; opinion (151)

wóénan *I* expect, hope for; suppose, think (151)

wóéninga *av.* possibly, perhaps (151)

wóépan (éo, éo, óé) *7* weep; lament (56)

ȝe-wóérgian *II* tire, weary (103)

wóérgu (?) *f.sg.* weariness, grief (?) (103)

wóériȝ *aj.* weary, tired (103)

wóésan *I* wet, soak (1)

wóéstan *I* lay waste, devastate (58)

wóéste *aj.* waste, desolate (58)

wóésten (~as; ~u) *m.n.* desert, wasteland (58)

wóéþ-ness *f.sg.* mildness (4)

Y

ýðian *II* billow, fluctuate (112)

yfel (~; yflu) *n.* evil (165)

yfel (wiersa, wier[re]st) *aj.* bad, evil, inferior (165)

~þweorh (?) *aj.* wickedly antagonistic (?) (4)

yfele (wiers, wierst) *av.* badly (165)

yfelian *II* injure, inflict evil upon (165)

yfemest *aj.av.* highest, uppermost (57)

ymb- *pref.* around, about (226)

~hoga (~n) *m.* anxiety, care, solicitude (571)

~hwyrft (~as) *m.* rotation; circle, circuit; environment, region; orb, world, firmament (207)

~lyt *m.sg.* expanse, circuit (1)

~sittend *m.pl.* neighboring peoples (495)

~útan *av.* about, around, without (231)

ymb(e) *prep.* around, by, about, near; after; on account of (226)

ymen (~as) *m.* hymn (2)

yplen (~u) *n.* top, height (267)

yppan *I* open up, manifest, reveal (267)

yppe *f.sg.* platform; high seat: *aj.* open, known, manifest (267)

ypping *f.sg.* mounting mass of water (?) (267)

ýr *m.sg.* yew-wood bow (?); iron axehead (?); name of Y-rune (4)

ysle (yslan) *f.* glowing ash, spark (4)

ýsope *f.sg.* hyssop (1)

ýst (~a) *f.* storm (14)

~iȝ *aj.* stormy (14)

ýstan *I* storm, rage (14)

ýtemest *aj.* uttermost, last (231)

ýþ (ýða) *f.* wave (112)

~hof (~u) *n.* wave-dwelling, ship (51)

~láf *f.sg.* what is left by the waves; sand; shore (78)

Z

zefferus *m.sg.* zephyr (1)

þ

þá *av.* then, at that time, after that: *cj.*
  when, since, as: þá . . . þá *correl.* when
  . . . then: *pron.*, *see* sé, sío, þæt (1692)
~ȝíen *av.* yet, still, further (70)
~ȝíet *av.* still, yet (93)
þaca (~n) *m.* roof (61)
ȝe-þafa *m.sg.* assenter; helper (13)
þafian *II* allow, consent, permit; en-
  dure, submit; approve, grant (13)
þáh *see* þíon
þan *see* þanne
þanc (~as) *m.* thought, mind, purpose,
  plan; favor, grace; pleasure, satis-
  faction; gratitude, thanks; reward
  (509)
~hycgende *ppl.aj.* thoughtful (571)
~word (~) *n.* thanks (631)
ȝe-þanc (~as; ~u) *m.n.* thought, mind,
  purpose (509)
þancian *II* thank; repay (509)
ȝe-þanc-metian *II* consider (146)
þancol *aj.* thoughtful; mindful; consider-
  ate; wise (509)
þancung (~a) *f.* thanksgiving (509)
þand *see* þindan
þanne/þan *av.* then, therefore, how-
  ever; as, just as: *cj.* then, when,
  whenever; since (956)
þanon(e) *av.* thence; afterwards; whence;
  thereupon (956)
þawian *II* thaw (1)
þĕ *indecl. rel. particle* who, which, what:
  enclitically sĕ-þe, *etc.*, he, she, it who,
  etc.: *cj.* when, then, where; or (10458)
þé *pers.pron.* (*dat.acc.sg.*) thee, you
  (15974)
þeah *see* þicgan
þéah *av.cj.* however, nevertheless; al-
  though, though (300)
~ná *cj.* nevertheless, however (377)

þeaht (~u) *f.n.* thought; knowledge;
  counsel; plan (509)
þeahtian *II* ponder (509)
-þeahtiende *ppl.suff.* deliberating (509)
þeahtung (~a) *f.* counsel; consideration
  (509)
þearf (~a) *f.* necessity, need, want;
  distress, trouble; advantage, benefit,
  utility (152)
~líće *av.* to good purpose (322)
þearf *see* þurfan
þearfa (~n) *m.* needy person, beggar:
  aj. in need of, lacking (152)
þearfende *ppl.aj.* needy, poor (152)
þearfian *II* need: ȝe~ necessitate (152)
þearl(e) *aj.av.* severe(ly), strong(ly) (46)
þéaw (~as) *m.* custom, manner, habit,
  usage, morality (56)
~fæst *aj.* honorable (372)
þeććan (þeahte) *I* cover, cover over;
  conceal, enclose, envelop (61)
þeććend *m.sg.* protector (61)
þećen *f.sg.* covering, roof (61)
þecgan *I* receive, consume: á~ receive:
  ȝe~ consume: of~ consume, destroy
  (49)
þégan *I* serve (87)
þeȝn (~as) *m.* servant, retainer; dis-
  ciple; royal officer, minister, thane;
  man, warrior (210)
~líće *av.* in manly fashion, as a thane
  should do (210)
~sciepe *m.sg.* service; bravery (340)
~sorg *f.sg.* sorrow for retainers (174)
þeȝnian *II* serve, minister to (210)
þeȝnung (~a) *f.* service; ministration,
  ceremonial (210)
þegu (þega) *f.* receiving, partaking (49)
þel (~u) *n.* floor, planking, deck (8)
þenćan (þohte) *I* think, consider, sup-
  pose: á~ think; plan: be~ think,
  consider; confide, entrust: for~ des-
  pair: ȝe~ think, consider, devise,
  plan; remember; care for: ȝeond~
  contemplate: ymb~ consider (509)

þenden *av.cj.* meanwhile, then; while, as long as, until (77)

þenġel *m.sg.* prince, ruler (52)

þennan (þenede) *I* stretch, extend (16)

þéod (~a) *f.* people, nation, troop, host: *pref.* of a people, national; great, vast, main, terrible (460)

~sciepe (-sciepas) *m.* people, nation; association, friendship; authority, due observance, law (340)

ʒe-þéode *n.sg.* nation; language (460)

þéoden (þéodnas) *m.* chieftain, prince, lord; the Lord: *pref.* of a chieftain; great, vast, main, terrible (460)

þéodisc *n.sg.* language (460)

þéof (~as) *m.* thief (7)

þéoh *n.sg.* thigh (1)

ʒé-þéon (-þéode) *I* do, perform (87)

þéostor *aj.* dark, gloomy (72)

þéotan (éa, u, o) *2* howl; sound forth (4)

þéow (~as) *m.* servant, slave: *aj.* servile (87)

þéowa (~n) *m.* servant (87)

þéowe/þéowen(e) *f.sg.* maidservant (87)

þéow(i)an *I-II* serve, minister to (87)

þéowot *n.sg.* service (87)

þerscan (æ, u, o) *3* thrash, beat (2)

þerscwold *m.sg.* threshold (2)

þes, þíos, þis *pron.aj.* this (507)

þicce *aj.av.* thick; thickly, frequently (11)

þicgan (þiʒede/þeah, þǽgon, þiʒed) *I-5* receive, partake of: for~(?) overeat: ʒe~ receive; drink: oþ~ take from, seize (49)

þider *av.* thither, there (34)

ʒe-þíedan *I* join, associate: oþ~ separate: under~ subjugate (15)

ʒe-þíede *aj.* good, generous (15)

þíestre (þíestru; ~) *f.n.* darkness, gloom (72)

á-þíestrian *II* grow dark (72)

á-þíetan *I* blow, sound (4)

ʒe-þíewe *aj.* usual, customary (56)

þiʒen *f.sg.* food (49)

þiʒnen *f.sg.* maidservant (210)

þindan (a, u, u) *3* swell, swell up, be angry; melt, pass away (4)

þing (~) *n.* thing, event, circumstance, condition; concern, affair; meeting, court (110)

~ʒe-mearc *n.sg.* period of time (73)

~rǽden *f.sg.* plea, pleading (174)

ʒe-þingan *I* determine, appoint; determine (to go to) (25)

ʒe-þinge (-þinġu) *n.* council; agreement, settlement; issue, result; fate (110)

þingian *II* speak, discourse, address; determine, settle; conciliate, intercede; supplicate (110)

þingum *av.dat.* purposely; strongly (110)

þíon [<*þíohan<*þíhan] (þáh, þungon, u) *1-3* prosper, profit, thrive: ʒe~ thrive, flourish, increase, ripen: ofer~ excel, surpass: on~ thrive; be of service (52)

þíos, þis *see* þes

þísle *f.sg.* shaft (of a cart) (1)

þistel (þistlas) *m.* thistle (2)

ʒe-þofta (~n) *m.* companion (2)

ʒe-þóht (~as) *m.* thought, mind (509)

þolian *II* endure, suffer; hold out; be without, lack, lose: á~ endure patiently (?); attain possession of, gain (?): for~ do without: ʒe~ endure, remain; lose (91)

þon/þý *art.instr.av.* the; any; for that reason; therefore (10458)

~lǽs *cj.* lest (123)

þorfte *see* þurfan

þorn (~as) *m.* thorn, thorn-bush; name of þ-rune (4)

þracu (þraca) *f.* attack, violence; power, force (41)

þrafian *II* compel; blame (2)

þrág (~a) *f.* time, occasion, season; hard time (57)

~mǽl (~) *n.* unhappy time (57)

~mǽlum *av.dat.* at times (57)

þrágum *av.dat.* at times (57)

þrang *see* þringan

ȝe-þrang (~) *n.* throng, crowd, tumult (64)

þréa (~) *m.f.n.* abuse, threat; punishment, oppression; calamity, violence; distress, misery, terror (45)

~níedla (~n) *m.* grievous stress (70)

~níed-líċ *aj.* calamitous (70)

þréa(ga)n (þréade) *I* rebuke, punish; threaten, afflict, oppress (17)

þréat (~as) *m.* warrior-band, troop, crowd; threat, punishment, calamity (69)

þréat *see* þréotan

þréatian *II* threaten, press, force; reprove, check (13)

á-þréotan (éa, u, o) *2* weary, tire of; displease, irk (6)

þrī- *pref.* three (104)

~milċe *n.sg.* May (time of thrice-daily milkings) (2)

~ness *f.sg.* the Holy Trinity (104)

~tiȝ *num.* thirty (24)

~wa *av.* thrice (104)

þridda *aj.* third (104)

þridian *II* deliberate (3)

þríe/þrío *num.* three (104)

~hund *num.* three hundred (60)

~rœ́ðre *aj.* having three banks of oars (4)

~teogoða *aj.* thirteenth (5)

~tíene *num.* thirteen (24)

þrindan (a, u, u) *3* swell (3)

ȝe-þring *n.sg.* press, throng, commotion (64)

þringan (a, u, u) *3* press forward, crowd, throng: á~ press out; press forward: be~ encompass: for~ utterly crush (?); force away from a position (?); ȝe~ press forward, throng; approach; oppress; swell up: on~ press forward; crack open: oþ~ deprive of: to~ drive asunder: ymb~ press about: æt~ deprive of (64)

þrintan (a, u, u) *3* swell (3)

þrío *see* þríe

þríste(e) *aj.av.* bold(ly), daring(ly), presumptuous(ly) (48)

þroht *m.sg.* affliction; toil: *aj.* laborious; dire (14)

~heard *aj.* patient (261)

~iȝ *aj.* persistent; laborious (14)

þrosm *m.sg.* smoke (6)

þroten *see* þréotan

þrówere (þróweras) *m.* sufferer, martyr (66)

þrówian *II* suffer, endure (66)

þrówung (~a) *f.* suffering; the Passion (66)

þrunten *see* þrintan

þryċċan *I* press upon, crowd in on: be~ press down: for~ oppress; overwhelm, torment: of~ seize, occupy (14)

ȝe-þrýðed *ppl.aj.* mighty (33)

þrýðiȝ *aj.* strong, powerful (33)

þrýðum *av.dat.* very; violently (33)

þrymm (~as) *m.* crowd, troop, host; force, tumult, violence; might, power, strength; glory, majesty, splendor (179)

~sittende *ppl.aj.* enthroned in glory (495)

þrymma (~n) *m.* hero (179)

þrymme/þrymmum *av.dat.* mightily; violently (179)

þrysm(i)an *I-II* grow dark, misty: á~ choke with smoke, suffocate (6)

þrýþ (þrýðe) *f.* force, might, strength; glory, majesty; multitude, troop, host (33)

~bord (~) *n.* mighty shield (?); mighty ship (?) (73)

þræc (þracu) *n.* throng, press, tumult (41)

þrǽd *m.sg.* thread (1)

þræft *n.sg.* contentiousness (2)

þrǽgan *I* run (4)

ȝe-þrǽstan *I* oppress, constrain (1)

þúf (~as) *m.* battle standard, banner of plumes (3)

þúhte *see* þyncan

þungen *ppl.aj.* prosperous, excellent, noble (52)

þungon *see* þíon

þunian *II* be stretched out, be prominent, be proud: on~ swell out, exceed due bounds (?) (16)

þunor *m.sg.* thunder (14)

~rád *f.sg.* thunder (56)

þunrian *II* thunder (14)

þun-wange (-wangan) *f.n.* temple (of the head) (16; 76)

ȝe-þuren *ppl.aj.* mixed together; forged: *cp.* þweran (13)

þurfan (þearf, þearft, þorfte) *prp.* need, be in need, have need; be obliged, have cause, have good reason (152)

þurh *av.* through, throughout: *prep.* through; by, during, from, in, with; because of, by reason of, by way of (664)

þurst *m.sg.* thirst (20)

~iȝ *aj.* thirsty, thirsting for (20)

þus *av.* thus, in this manner, so (74)

þúsend (~u) *num.* thousand (33)

~mǽlum *av.dat.* by thousands (57)

þuton *see* þéotan

ȝe-þuxian *II* become dark (1)

þwéal (~) *n.* washing, bath; soap, ointment (5)

þwéan [<*þweahan <*þwahan] (þwóg, ó, þwæȝen) *6* wash, cleanse (5)

þweorh *aj.* transverse, crosswise; perverse (4)

~tíeme *aj.* obstinate, perverse (13)

~timber *aj.* resolutely made (39)

þweran (æ, ǽ, o) *4* soften, render malleable, forge; beat, mix together (13)

ȝe-þwing *n.sg.* confinement, restraint (1)

þwítan (á, i, i) *1* cut, whittle (1)

þwóg *see* þwéan

þwæȝen *see* þwéan

ȝe-þwǽnan *I* moisten, soften (5)

ȝe-þwǽre *aj.* united, in accord; gentle, peaceful (13)

ȝe-þwǽrian *II* reconcile; soften (13)

þý *see* þon

ȝe-þyhte *aj.* profitable, serviceable (?) (52)

þýhtiȝ *aj.* strong, doughty, bold (52)

ȝe-þyld (~a) *f.* patience (21)

~iȝ *aj.* patient (21)

ȝe-þyldum *av.dat.* steadily (21)

þyle *m.sg.* orator, spokesman (2)

þyl-líc *see* þys-líc

þyncan (þúhte) *I* seem, appear: of~ be displeasing (509)

ȝe-þynȝþu (-þynȝþa) *f.* dignity, honor (52)

þynne *aj.* thin (16)

þynnung (~a) *f.* thinning (16)

þýrel (~u) *n.* aperture: *aj.* pierced through (664)

~wamb *aj.* with pierced belly (14)

þyrnen *aj.* thorny (4)

þyrran *I* make or become dry (2)

þyrre *aj.* dry (2)

þyrs *m.sg.* giant; demon (3)

þyrstan *I* be thirsty, thirst after: of~ be very thirsty, avidly desirous (20)

þys-líc/þyl-líc *aj.* such (74)

þyssa (~n) *m.* rusher, that which rushes (8)

þysse (þyssan) *f.* violence (?) (8)

þýwan *I* press, oppress; force, urge, threaten: ȝe~ oppress, crush, subjugate (87)

þæc (þacu) *n.* roof (61)

þæcelle *f.sg.* torch, light (61)

þǽgon *see* þicgan

þǽr *av.* there, then; would that: *cj.* where, when, if (972)

þæs *av.* afterwards, thereafter, therefore; to that degree or extent (10458)

þæt, ~te *cj.* that, so that; until; pro-

þæt

vided that, in order that; because (10458)

þæt *see* sé, sío, þæt

Æ

ǽ/ǽw *f.sg.* law; rite; marriage; the (Old, New) Law or Testament (64)

~lǽrend (~) *m.* doctor of the law (198)

~wita (~n) *m.* councilor, scholar (764)

ǽ- *pref.* (*inceptive, perfective, privative*; *cp.* á-) (25)

~byl3 (~) *n.* anger (36)

~bylgþ *f.sg.* anger; offense (36)

~3íepe *aj.* awkward, not clever (1)

~menn *aj.* uninhabited (1030)

~metti3/ǽmti3 *aj.* empty (298)

~miell-ness (~a) *f.* insipidity; sloth (2)

~mynd *f.sg.* forgetfulness, neglect (?); jealousy, malice (?) (419)

~rist *m.f.n.* resurrection (120)

~swic (~as) *m.* offense, infamy (64)

æcer (~as) *m.* arable land, (cultivated) field (5)

æcs (~a) *f.* axe (1)

ǽder/ǽdre (ǽdra; ǽdran) *f.* vein, artery: *pl.* streams (11)

ǽdre *av.* quickly (29)

æðele *aj.* noble (379)

3e-æðele *aj.* inborn, natural (379)

æðelian *II* ennoble (379)

æðeling (~as) *m.* nobleman, prince (of the realm) (379)

æðelu *f.n.pl.* nobility, lineage (379)

ǽðm (~as) *m.* breath (2)

æf- *pref.* (*separative or perfective; accented form of* of-) (8)

~lást (~as) *m.* changed course (?); a wandering from the course (?) (72)

~þanca (~n) *m.* displeasure; grudge; offense (509)

~þunca *m.sg.* offense, vexation (509)

~œst (~e) *f.* disfavor, dislike; malice (31)

ǽfen (~) *n.* evening, eve, day before (34)

ǽfre *av.* ever, always (296)

æftan *av.* after, behind (386)

æfter *av.prep.* after; about, along, concerning, on, through; according to, on account of (386)

æfterra *aj.* second, following, next (386)

ǽ3 (~ru) *n.* egg (3)

ǽ3- *pref.* (*generalizes meaning of pronouns & adverbs*) (125)

~hwá *pron.* anyone (521)

~hwanan *av.* from anywhere (11)

~hwelć *pron.* each, everyone (477)

~hwider *av.* in all directions (9)

~hwæðer *pron.av.* each, either, both (186)

~hwǽr *av.* anywhere, everywhere (136)

~hwæs *av.* completely (521)

ǽgnian *see* ágnian

ǽht (~e) *f.* property, possessions (370)

ǽl (~as) *m.* eel (1)

æl- *pref.* all, completely (1600)

ǽlan *I* burn; kindle (33)

ǽlć *aj.pron.* each, every, all (40)

ǽled *m.sg.* fire, burning up (33)

ǽling (~e) *f.* burning, ardor (33)

ælmes-3eorn *aj.* benevolent (228)

ælmesse (ælmessan) *f.* alms, alms-giving (6)

ælmes-selen *f.sg.* alms-giving (276)

ǽne *av.* once (850)

ǽni3 *aj.pron.* any, any one (850)

ǽninga *av.* completely, altogether (850)

ǽn-líć *aj.* unique, noble, splendid (322)

æppel (æpplas) *m.* apple (13)

~fealu *aj.* apple-colored, bay (23)

æpplede *aj.* rounded, circular, embossed (13)

ǽr (~) *n.* brass (5)

ǽr *av.* before, formerly, previously; early: *prep.* before: *cj.* before, before that (649)

~est *superl.aj.av.* first; at first (649)

ǽr- *pref.* fore-, ancient, early, former; premature (649)

~glæd *aj.* long-fortunate (?) (39)

~gód *aj.* pre-eminent (401)

~ing *f.sg.* daybreak (1)

ǽren *aj.* brazen (5)

ǽrende (ǽrendu) *n.* message, errand (33)

ǽrendian *II* take a message; intercede (33)

ǽrn (~) *n.* building; chamber (18)

ǽrnan *I* ride, hasten (41)

ǽror *comp.av.* before, earlier, sooner, rather: *prep.* before (649)

ǽrra *comp.aj.* earlier, former (649)

ǽs *n.sg.* carrion (4)

æsc (~as) *m.* ash-wood, ash-wood spear; name of Æ-rune and ligature æ (28)

ǽsce (ǽscan) *f.* inquiry (16)

æt *prep.* at, near, in; as to; from, at the hands of (375)

~féle *m.sg.* attachment, devotion (20)

~foran *av.prep.* to the fore, forward, in front of, before (223)

~grǽpe *aj.* seizing, at grips with (58)

~gǽdre *av.* together (86)

~hwá *pron.* each (521)

~rihte *aj.av.* present, close at hand; immediately (417)

~samne *av.* together (221).

~steall *m.sg.* camp, battle-station (16)

~wist *f.sg.* presence (4189)

ǽt *m.f.n.* food; eating (65)

ǽt *see* etan

ǽtren *aj.* poisonous; malefic (55)

ǽw *see* ǽ

ǽwan *I* despise, scorn (6)

ǽwisc *f.sg.* disgrace, shame (6)

Œ

œ́ċe/éċe *aj.av.* eternal(ly) (419)

œ́ċ-ness *f.* eternity (419)

œ́ðel (œ́ðlas) *m.* inherited estate, native land; dwelling; name of Œ-, later of long E-rune (161)

~boda *m.sg.* native preacher (209)

~léas *aj.* exiled (224)

~riht *n.sg.* ancestral rights, possessions (417)

~stæf *m.sg.* heir, successor (40)

œ́ðian *II* breathe, exhale, rise up; smell (2)

œfstan *I* hasten (56)

on-œ́ʒan *I* fear; frighten (218)

œ́ht *f.sg.* hostility, pursuit (22)

~ness (~a) *f.* persecution (22)

œ́htan *I* follow after, persecute (22)

œ́htend (~) *m.* persecutor (22)

œle *m.sg.* (olive) oil (6)

œ́st (~e) *f.* favor, legacy; gift, treasure; grace, kindness (31)

~iʒ *aj.* gracious, kindly (31)

œ́ste *aj.* gracious (31)

œ́stum *av.dat.* kindly, with good will (31)

Lightning Source UK Ltd.
Milton Keynes UK
UKHW030613210722
406167UK00006B/670

9 781442 651869